The Supporters' Guide to Scottish Football 2001

EDITOR
John Robinson

Ninth Edition

SOCCER BOOKS LIMITED sell the largest range of new and used English-language Football books and videos anywhere in the world. With almost 800 new books and 300 videos, our mail order business is the World leader.

For a full list write to the address below or visit our web site as shown.

British Library Cataloguing in Publication Data
A catalogue record for this book is available from the British Library

ISBN 1-86223-046-3

The Publishers, and the Football Clubs itemised are unable to accept liability for any loss, damage or injury caused by error or inaccuracy in the information published in this guide.

Printed by The Cromwell Press

FOREWORD

We wish to thank the club secretaries of the Scottish Premier League, the Scottish League, the Highland League and the East of Scotland League for their assistance in providing the information contained in this guide. We also wish to thank Bob Budd (cover artwork), Chris Ambler, Owen Pavey & Kevin Norminton (photos), David Thomson (Scottish Football League), J.H. Grant (Highland League) and J.M. Greenhorn (East of Scotland League) for their valuable assistance.

This year we have expanded the information about East of Scotland League clubs to include ground photographs and more extensive information

When using this guide, readers should note that most clubs also extend the child concessionary prices to include Senior Citizens.

Finally, we would like to wish our readers a happy and safe spectating season.

John Robinson
EDITOR

CONTENTS

HAMPDEN –
SCOTLAND'S NATIONAL STADIUM

Opened: 1903
Location: Hampden Park, Mount Florida, Glasgow   G42 9BA
Telephone Nº: (0141) 332-6372

Record Attendance: 150,239 (Scotland vs England, 17th April 1937)
Pitch Size: 115 × 75 yards
Ground Capacity: 52,145 (All seats)

GENERAL INFORMATION
Car Parking: Car Park for 600 cars at the Stadium
Coach Parking: Stadium Car Park
Nearest Railway Station: Mount Florida and King's Park (both 5 minutes walk)
Nearest Bus Station: Buchanan Street
Nearest Police Station: Aikenhead Road, Glasgow
Police Telephone Nº: (0141) 532-4900

DISABLED INFORMATION
Wheelchairs: Accommodated in disabled spectators sections at all levels in the South Stand, particularly levels 1 and 4 where special catering and toilet facilities are available.
Disabled Toilets: Available
Commentaries are available for the blind + a CCTV link with commentary for other disabled supporters
Contact: (0141) 332-6372

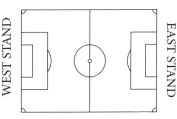

NORTH STAND

WEST STAND

EAST STAND

SOUTH STAND

Travelling Supporters' Information:
Routes: From the South: Take the A724 to the Cambuslang Road and at Eastfield branch left into Main Street and follow through Burnhill Street and Westmuir Place into Prospecthill Road. Turn left into Aikenhead Road and right into Mount Annan for Kinghorn Drive and the Stadium; From the South: Take the A77 Fenwick Road, through Kilmarnock Road into Pollokshaws Road then turn right into Langside Avenue. Pass through Battle Place to Battlefield Road and turn left into Cathcart Road. Turn right into Letherby Drive, right into Carmunnock Road and 1st left into Mount Annan Drive for the Stadium; From the North & East: Exit M8 Junction 15 and passing Infirmary on left proceed into High Street and cross the Albert Bridge into Crown Street. Join Cathcart Road and proceed South until it becomes Carmunnock Road. Turn left into Mount Annan Drive and left again into Kinghorn Drive for the Stadium.

THE SCOTTISH
FOOTBALL ASSOCIATION

Founded
1873

Address
6 Park Gardens, Glasgow   G3 7YF

Phone
(0141) 332-6372

THE SCOTTISH
FOOTBALL LEAGUE

Founded
1890

Address
188 West Regent Street, Glasgow   G2 4RY

Phone
(0141) 248-3844

ABERDEEN FC

Founded: 1903 (**Entered League:** 1904)	**Colours:** Shirts – Red
Former Names: None	Shorts – Red
Nickname: 'The Dons'	**Telephone N°:** (01224) 650400
Ground: Pittodrie Stadium, Pittodrie	**Ticket Office:** (01224) 632328
Street, Aberdeen AB24 5QH	**Fax Number:** (01224) 644173
Record Attendance: 45,061 (13/3/54)	**Ground Capacity:** 22,199 (all seats)
Pitch Size: 109 × 71 yards	

MERKLAND STAND
FAMILY ENCLOSURE

SOUTH STAND

SOUTH STAND
EAST (Away)

(PITTODRIE STREET)
MAIN STAND

RICHARD DONALD STAND
GOLF ROAD

GENERAL INFORMATION

Supporters Club: Susan Scott, Aldon, Wellington Road, Aberdeen   AB1 4BJ
Telephone N°: (01224) 898260
Car Parking: Beach Boulevard, King Street & Golf Road
Coach Parking: Beach Boulevard
Nearest Railway Station: Aberdeen (1 mile)
Nearest Bus Station: Aberdeen
Club Shop: AFC Direct , Bridge Street, Aberdeen
Opening Times: 9.00am to 5.30pm
Telephone N°: (01224) 405305
Postal Sales: Yes
Nearest Police Station: Aberdeen
Police Telephone N°: (01224) 639111

GROUND INFORMATION

Away Supporters' Entrances & Sections:
Park Road entrance for the South Stand East

ADMISSION INFO (2000/2001 PRICES)

Adult Seating: £15.00 to £25.00
Child Seating: £1.00 to £25.00
Additional Child discounts apply – Prices vary according to the category of the game
Programme Price: £2.00

DISABLED INFORMATION

Wheelchairs: 26 spaces available in front of the Richard Donald Stand & Merkland Stand
Helpers: One helper admitted per wheelchair
Prices: Free of charge for the disabled. Helpers charged concessionary prices
Disabled Toilets: One available in Richard Donald Stand and one is available by the Merkland Stand
Are Bookings Necessary: Yes
Contact: (01224) 650423

Web site: www.afc.co.uk

Travelling Supporters' Information:
Routes: From the City Centre, travel along Union Street then turn left into King Street. The Stadium is about ½ mile along King Street (A92) on the right-hand side.

AIRDRIEONIANS FC

Founded: 1878 (**Entered League:** 1903)
Former Names: Excelsior FC
Nickname: 'Diamonds'
Ground: Shyberry Excelsior Stadium,
Broomfield Park, Craigneuk Avenue,
Airdrie   ML6 8QZ
Pitch Size: 115 × 75 yards

Colours: Shirts – White with Red Diamond
     Shorts – Red
Telephone Nº: (01236) 622000
Ticket Office: (01236) 622000
Fax Number: (01236) 626002
Ground Capacity: 10,156 (All seats)

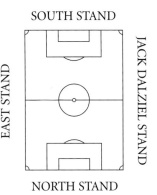

SOUTH STAND

EAST STAND

JACK DALZIEL STAND

NORTH STAND

GENERAL INFORMATION

Supporters Club: David Johnstone, 16 Deveron
Street, Coatbridge
Telephone Nº: (01236) 423812
Car Parking: Behind all the Stands
Coach Parking: Behind the East Stand
Nearest Railway Station: Airdrie (1½ miles)
Nearest Bus Station: Gartlea – Airdrie Town Centre
Club Shop: 93 Graham Street, Airdrie & at ground
Opening Times: Graham Street: Weekdays 9.00am to
5.00pm. Saturdays 9.00am to 4.00pm. Closed for lunch
12.30pm to 1.30pm. Ground: Opens 1 hour before matches
Telephone Nº: (01236) 747255
Postal Sales: Yes
Nearest Police Station: Anderson Street, Airdrie
Police Telephone Nº: (01236) 762222

GROUND INFORMATION

Away Supporters' Entrances & Sections:
East and South Stands

ADMISSION INFO (1999/2000 PRICES)

Adult Seating: £12.00
Child Seating: £7.00
One adult and one child: £16.00
Programme Price: £1.50

DISABLED INFORMATION

Wheelchairs: Spaces available for home and away
fans accommodated in the front sections
Helpers: One admitted per disabled supporter
Prices: Free for the disabled. Helpers half-price
Disabled Toilets: Available in all the stands
Are Bookings Necessary: Preferable
Contact: (01236) 622000

Web site: www.airdrieoniansfc.com

Travelling Supporters' Information:
Routes: From the East: Exit the M8 at Junction 6 and take the A73 (signposted Cumbernauld). Pass through
Chapelhall into Airdrie and turn right into Petersburn Road – the ground is on the left; From the West: Take the
A8 to the Chapelhall turn-off for Chapelhall. Join the A73 at Chapelhall, then as above.

ALBION ROVERS FC

Founded: 1882 **(Entered League:** 1903)
Former Names: None
Nickname: 'Wee Rovers'
Ground: Cliftonhill Stadium, Main Street,
Coatbridge, Lanarkshire   ML5 3RB
Record Attendance: 27,381 (8/2/36)
Pitch Size: 110 × 72 yards

Colours: Shirts – Yellow with Red Trim
Shorts – Yellow
Telephone Nº: (01236) 606334
Ticket Office: (01236) 607041
Fax Number: (01236) 606334
Ground Capacity: 2,496
Seating Capacity: 538

WEST END

MAIN STREET GRANDSTAND (Away)

CAR PARK ALBION STREET

EAST END

Disabled Area

GENERAL INFORMATION

Supporters Club: None
Telephone Nº: –
Car Parking: Street Parking and Albion Street
Coach Parking: Albion Street
Nearest Railway Station: Coatdyke (10 mins. walk)
Nearest Bus Station: Coatbridge
Club Shop: At ground
Opening Times: One hour before each home match
Telephone Nº: (01236) 606334
Postal Sales: Yes
Nearest Police Station: Coatbridge (½ mile)
Police Telephone Nº: (01236) 50200

GROUND INFORMATION

Away Supporters' Entrances & Sections:
Main Street entrance for the Main Street Area

ADMISSION INFO (2000/2001 PRICES)

Adult Standing: £6.00
Adult Seating: £7.00
Child Standing: £3.00
Child Seating: £4.00
Children under the age of 12 are admitted free
Programme Price: £1.00

DISABLED INFORMATION

Wheelchairs: Approximately 30 spaces available in the Disabled Area
Helpers: Please phone the club for information
Prices: Please phone the club for information
Disabled Toilets: One available at the East End of the Ground
Are Bookings Necessary: No, but preferred
Contact: (01236) 606334

Travelling Supporters' Information:
Routes: From East or West: Take the A8/M8 to the Shawhead Interchange then follow the A725 to the Town Centre. Take A89 signs towards Airdrie at the roundabout, the ground is then on the left; From the South: Take the A725 from Bellshill/Hamilton/Motherwell/M74 to Coatbridge. Take A89 signs towards Airdrie at the roundabout, the ground is then on the left; From North: Take A73 to Airdrie then follow signs for A8010 to Coatbridge. Join the A89 and the ground is one mile on the right.

ALLOA ATHLETIC FC

Founded: 1878 (**Entered League**: 1921)	**Colours**: Shirts – Gold and Black
Former Names: None	Shorts – Black
Nickname: 'The Wasps'	**Telephone Nº**: (01259) 722695
Ground: Recreation Park, Clackmannan	**Ticket Office**: (01259) 722695
Road, Alloa FK10 1RY	**Fax Number**: (01259) 210886
Record Attendance: 13,000 (26/2/39)	**Ground Capacity**: 3,148
Pitch Size: 110 × 75 yards	**Seating Capacity**: 424

CLACKMANNAN ROAD

HILTON ROAD

MAIN STAND

GENERAL INFORMATION
Supporters Club: R. Snaddon, c/o Club
Telephone Nº: (01259) 722695
Car Parking: A Car Park is adjacent to the Ground
Coach Parking: By Police Direction
Nearest Railway Station: Stirling (7 miles)
Nearest Bus Station: Alloa
Club Shop: At ground
Opening Times: Matchdays only 1.30pm to 5.00pm
Telephone Nº: (01259) 722695
Postal Sales: Yes
Nearest Police Station: Alloa (½ mile)
Police Telephone Nº: (01259) 723255

GROUND INFORMATION
Away Supporters' Entrances & Sections:
Hilton Road entrance for the Hilton Road Side and
Clackmannan Road End

ADMISSION INFO (2000/2001 PRICES)
Adult Standing: £9.00
Adult Seating: £10.00
Child Standing: £5.00
Child Seating: £6.00
Programme Price: £1.50

DISABLED INFORMATION
Wheelchairs: Accommodated in the Disabled
Section underneath the Main Stand
Helpers: Admitted
Prices: Free of charge for the disabled and helpers
Disabled Toilets: One available in the Main Stand
Are Bookings Necessary: No
Contact: (01259) 722695

Travelling Supporters' Information:
Routes: From the South & East: Take the M74 to the M80 and exit at Junction 9 following the A907 into Alloa.
Continue over two roundabouts passing the brewery and Town Centre. The Ground is on the left-hand side of
the road.

ARBROATH FC

Founded: 1878 (**Entered League:** 1902)	**Colours:** Shirts – Maroon + White & Sky Blue
Former Names: None	Shorts – White with Maroon trim
Nickname: 'The Red Lichties'	**Telephone Nº:** (01241) 872157
Ground: Gayfield Park, Arbroath	**Ticket Office:** (01241) 872157
DD11 1QB	**Fax Number:** (01241) 431125
Record Attendance: 13,510 (23/2/52)	**Ground Capacity:** 6,488
Pitch Size: 115 × 71 yards	**Seating Capacity:** 715

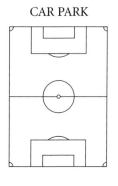

CAR PARK

QUEEN'S DRIVE   DUNDEE ROAD

GENERAL INFORMATION

Supporters Club: Mike Leonard, 31 Clova Avenue, Arbroath
Telephone Nº: (01241) 878293
Car Parking: Car Park in Queen's Drive
Coach Parking: Car Park in Queen's Drive
Nearest Railway Station: Arbroath (15 mins. walk)
Nearest Bus Station: Arbroath (10 minutes walk)
Club Shop: Premier Sports, West Port, Arbroath
Opening Times: Monday-Saturday 9.00am-5.00pm
Telephone Nº: (01241) 872838
Postal Sales: Yes
Nearest Police Station: Arbroath
Police Telephone Nº: (01241) 872222

GROUND INFORMATION

Away Supporters' Entrances & Sections:
None specifically unless it is an all-ticket game, in which case the Queen's Drive End is for Away fans

ADMISSION INFO (2000/2001 PRICES)

Adult Standing: £8.00
Adult Seating: £9.00
Child Standing: £4.00
Child Seating: £5.00
Programme Price: £1.20

DISABLED INFORMATION

Wheelchairs: 10 spaces available at the West End of the Main Stand
Helpers: Admitted
Prices: Normal prices for the disabled and helpers
Disabled Toilets: One available by the Club Shop
Are Bookings Necessary: Yes
Contact: (01241) 872157

Web site: www.arbroathfc.co.uk

Travelling Supporters' Information:
Routes: From Dundee and the West: Take the A92 (Coast Road). On entering Arbroath, pass under the Railway Line and the ground is on the right-hand side; From Stonehaven/Montrose: Take the A92, pass through Arbroath and past the Harbour and the ground is on the left-hand side.

AYR UNITED FC

Founded: 1910 (**Entered League:** 1910)
Former Names: Ayr Parkhouse FC
& Ayr FC (amalgamated in 1910)
Nickname: 'The Honest Men'
Ground: Somerset Park, Tryfield Place,
Ayr   KA8 9NB
Record Attendance: 25,225 (13/9/69)
Pitch Size: 110 × 72 yards

Colours: Shirts – White
Shorts – Black
Telephone Nº: (01292) 263435/263436
Ticket Office: (01292) 263435/263436
Fax Number: (01292) 281314
Ground Capacity: 9,941
Seating Capacity: 1,500

GENERAL INFORMATION

Supporters Club: c/o Club
Telephone Nº: (01292) 263435
Car Parking: Craigie Car Park, Ayr Racecourse and
Somerset Road Car Park
Coach Parking: Craigie Car Park
Nearest Railway Station: Ayr or Newton-on-Ayr
(both stations are 10 minutes walk)
Nearest Bus Station: Sandgate, Ayr
Club Shop: At the Ground
Opening Times: Weekdays 8.30am to 5.30pm
Home matchdays 11.00am to 3.00pm
Telephone Nº: (01292) 263435/263436
Postal Sales: Yes
Nearest Police Station: King Street, Ayr (½ mile)
Police Telephone Nº: (01292) 664000

GROUND INFORMATION

Away Supporters' Entrances & Sections:
Turnstiles 1-7 for the Railway End (covered terrace)

+ turnstiles 9-10 for Main Stand accommodation

ADMISSION INFO (2000/2001 PRICES)

Adult Standing: £10.00
Adult Seating: £13.00
Child/Senior Citizen Standing: £5.00
Child Seating: In the Family Stand only – 1 Adult +
1 Child for £12.00 (each additional child is £5.00)
Programme Price: £1.50

DISABLED INFORMATION

Wheelchairs: 24 spaces are available in the Disabled
Area beneath the Family Stand
Helpers: One admitted per wheelchair
Prices: Free for one wheelchair plus helper
Disabled Toilets: 2 Gents and 1 Ladies available in
the Disabled Area
Are Bookings Necessary: Only for all-ticket games
Contact: (01292) 263435/263436

Travelling Supporters' Information:
Routes: Make for A77 Ring Road around Ayr, exit via Whitletts Roundabout onto the A719 and follow road towards Ayr. Just past the end of the racecourse, turn right at traffic lights into Burnett Terrace, sharp left and right takes you into Somerset Road. (For car parking on Matchdays turn left at traffic lights and then right 50 yards on into Craigie Park or on Somerset Road just past the ground on the left into Somerset Road car park).

BERWICK RANGERS FC

Founded: 1881 (**Entered League:** 1951)
Former Names: None
Nickname: 'The Borderers'
Ground: Shielfield Park, Shielfield Terrace,
Tweedmouth, Berwick-upon-Tweed TD15 2EF
Record Attendance: 13,365 (28/1/67)
Pitch Size: 110 × 70 yards

Colours: Shirts – Black and Gold Stripes
Shorts – Black
Telephone Nº: (01289) 307424
Ticket Office: (01289) 307424
Fax Number: (01289) 307424
Ground Capacity: 4,131
Seating Capacity: 1,366

SHIELFIELD TERRACE

POPULAR SIDE TERRACING (Away)

MAIN STAND (All Seats) (CAR PARK)

GENERAL INFORMATION

Supporters Club Shop: Gordon Dickson,
19 Greenwood, Tweedmouth, Berwick-upon-Tweed
Telephone Nº: (01289) 308317
Car Parking: Large Car Park at the Ground
Coach Parking: Car Park at the Ground
Nearest Railway Station: Berwick-upon-Tweed (1½ miles)
Nearest Bus Station: Berwick Town Centre (1 mile)
Club Shop: At the Supporters' Club in the Ground
Opening Times: Matchdays Only
Telephone Nº: (01289) 307424
Postal Sales: Yes – via Supporters' Club at Ground
Nearest Police Station: Church Street (1 mile)
Police Telephone Nº: (01289) 307111

GROUND INFORMATION

Away Supporters' Entrances & Sections:
Shielfield Terrace entrance for Popular Side Terrace

ADMISSION INFO (2000/2001 PRICES)

Adult Standing: £8.00
Adult Seating: £8.00
Concessions: £4.00
Programme Price: £1.00

DISABLED INFORMATION

Wheelchairs: Accommodated in the Main Stand
Helpers: Admitted with wheelchair disabled
Prices: Concessionary prices apply to the disabled
Disabled Toilets: Available in the General Toilet Block and also in the Club Offices
Are Bookings Necessary: Yes
Contact: (01289) 307424 or 307623

Web site: www.brfc.mcmail.com

Travelling Supporters' Information:
Routes: From the North: Take the A1 (Berwick Bypass), cross new road-bridge then at roundabout take 1st exit. Carry on for approximately ¼ mile to the next roundabout, go straight across then continue approximately ¼ mile into Shielfield Terrace. Turn left and the ground is on the left; From South: Take A1 Bypass and continue across the first roundabout towards Screnerston/Tweedmouth and then on for 1 mile. At the crossroads/junction take 'Spittal' Road (right) and continue for approximately 1 mile until the road becomes Shielfield Terrace. The ground is on the left in Shielfield Terrace.

BRECHIN CITY FC

Founded: 1906 **(Entered League:** 1923)
Former Names: None
Nickname: 'The City'
Ground: Glebe Park, Trinity Road,
Brechin, Angus DD9 6BJ
Record Attendance: 8,244 (3/2/73)
Pitch Size: 110 × 76 yards

Colours: Shirts – Red and White
Shorts – Red and White
Telephone Nº: (01356) 622856
Ticket Office: (01356) 622856
Fax Number: (01356) 625667
Secretary's Number: (01356) 625691
Ground Capacity: 3,900
Seating Capacity: 1,518

COVERED TERRACING

TERRACING

STAND

TRINITY ROAD
SEATED ENCLOSURE

GENERAL INFORMATION
Supporters Club: c/o Glebe Park
Telephone Nº: (01356) 622856
Car Parking: Small Car Park at the Ground and
Street Parking
Coach Parking: Street Parking
Nearest Railway Station: Montrose (8 miles)
Nearest Bus Station: Brechin
Club Shop: At ground
Opening Times: Matchdays Only
Telephone Nº: (01356) 622856
Postal Sales: Yes
Nearest Police Station: Brechin (400 yards)
Police Telephone Nº: (01356) 622222

GROUND INFORMATION
Away Supporters' Entrances & Sections:
No segregation usually

ADMISSION INFO (2000/2001 PRICES)
Adult Standing: £7.00
Adult Seating: £7.00
Child Standing: £3.50
Child Seating: £3.50
Programme Price: £1.00

DISABLED INFORMATION
Wheelchairs: 10 spaces each available for home and
away fans
Helpers: Please phone the club for details
Prices: Please phone the club for details
Disabled Toilets: 2 available in Covered Enclosure
Are Bookings Necessary: No
Contact: (01356) 622856

Web site: www.brechincity.co.uk

Travelling Supporters' Information:
Routes: From the South and West: Take the M90 to the A94 and continue along past the first 'Brechin' turn-off.
Take the second turn signposted 'Brechin'. On entering Brechin, the ground is on the left-hand side of the road
between some houses.

CELTIC FC

Founded: 1888 **(Entered League:** 1890)
Former Names: None
Nickname: 'The Bhoys' 'The Hoops'
Ground: Celtic Park, Glasgow, G40 3RE
Record Attendance: 92,000 (1/1/38)
Pitch Size: 120 × 74 yards

Colours: Shirts – Green & White Hoops
Shorts – White
Telephone Nº: (0141) 556-2611
Ticket Office: (0141) 551-8653
Fax Number: (0141) 551-8106
Ground Capacity: 60,506 (All seats)

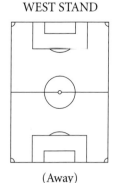

WEST STAND

LONDON ROAD SOUTH STAND

(JANEFIELD STREET) NORTH STAND

(Away)
EAST STAND

GENERAL INFORMATION

Supporters Club: Celtic Supporters' Association, Barrowfield Ground, 1524 London Road, Glasgow, G40 3RJ
Telephone Nº: (0141) 556-1882
Car Parking: Limited on Matchdays to those with a Valid Car Park Pass. Otherwise, street parking
Coach Parking: Gallowgate, Fielden Street, Biggar Street and Nuneaton Street
Nearest Railway Station: Bellgrove (10 mins. walk)
Nearest Bus Stop: Outside of the ground
Club Shop: Superstore at Celtic Park. Celtic shops also at Level 1 of North Stand; 21 High Street, Glasgow; 40 Dundas Street, Glasgow; Level 1, Jervis Centre, Dublin
Opening Times: Superstore: Mon-Sat 9am-6pm. Sundays 10am-5pm; North Stand: 2 hours before kick-off & half-time; High Street: Mon-Sat 9.30-5.30. Sun. 11.30-4.30; Dundas Street: Mon-Sat 9-5; Dublin Shop: Mon-Sat at least 9.30-6.00 (later on some days). Also open Sundays 12.00pm–6.00pm
Telephone Nº: (0141) 554-4231 (Superstore)
Mail-Order Sales: Yes – (0141) 550-1888

Nearest Police Station: London Road (½ mile)
Police Telephone Nº: (0141) 532-4600

GROUND INFORMATION
Away Supporters' Entrances & Sections:
Kinloch Street Turnstiles for the East Stand

ADMISSION INFO (2000/2001 PRICES)
Adult Seating: £19.00 – £25.00
Child Seating: £11.00 – £12.00
Programme Price: £2.00

DISABLED INFORMATION
Wheelchairs: 136 spaces for home fans and 6 spaces for away fans in the North Stand and East Stand
Helpers: 90 helpers admitted home fans, 6 for away
Prices: £8.00 – subject to availability (waiting list). This coverss a disabled fan and a helper
Disabled Toilets: 5 available in the North Stand, 2 in the East Stand and 3 in the South West Stand
Contact: (0141) 551-4311 (bookings are necessary)

Web site: www.celticfc.co.uk

Travelling Supporters' Information:
Routes: From the South and East: Take the A74 London Road towards the City Centre, Celtic Park is on the right about ½ mile past the Belvidere Hospital and the ground is clearly visible; From the West: Take the A74 London Road from the City Centre and turn left about ½ mile past Bridgeton Station.

CLYDE FC

Founded: 1878 (**Entered League:** 1906)
Former Names: None
Nickname: 'Bully Wee'
Ground: Broadwood Stadium,
Cumbenauld, Glasgow G68 9NE
Record Attendance: 8,000 (14/8/96)
Pitch Size: 115 × 75 yards

Colours: Shirts – White + Red & Black
Shorts – Black
Telephone Nº: (01236) 451511
Ticket Office: (01236) 451511
Fax Number: (01236) 733490
Ground Capacity: 8,200 (all seats)

GENERAL INFORMATION
Supporters Club: None
Telephone Nº: –
Car Parking: Behind the Main and West Stands
Coach Parking: Behind the Main Stand
Nearest Railway Station: Croy (1½ miles)
Nearest Bus Station: Cumbernauld Town Centre
Club Shop: At ground
Opening Times: One hour before a match and after the match
Telephone Nº: (01236) 451511
Postal Sales: Yes
Nearest Police Station: South Muirhead Street, Cumbernauld
Police Telephone Nº: (01236) 736085

GROUND INFORMATION
Away Supporters' Entrances & Sections:
West Stand Turnstile for the West Stand area

ADMISSION INFO (2000/2001 PRICES)
Adult Seating: £11.00
Child/Senior Citizen Seating: £5.00
Programme Price: £1.50

DISABLED INFORMATION
Wheelchairs: 10 spaces each for home and away fans accommodated in front sections of each stand
Helpers: One helper admitted per wheelchair
Prices: Free of charge for the disabled
Disabled Toilets: 4 available in Main & West Stands
Are Bookings Necessary: No
Contact: (01236) 451511

Web site: www.clydefc.co.uk

Travelling Supporters' Information:
Routes: From all Parts: Exit the A80 at Broadwood Junction and follow the signs for Broadwood. The Ground is signposted from the next roundabout.

CLYDEBANK FC

Founded: 1965 (**Entered League:** 1966)
Former Names: None
Nickname: 'The Bankies'
Ground: Cappielow Park, Sinclair Street,
Greenock PA15 2TY
Office Address: c/o West of Scotland RFC,
Burnbrae, Milngavie, Glasgow G62 6HX
Record Attendance: 18,000 (2/3/57)

Pitch Size: 110 × 71 yards
Colours: Shirts – Red and White Stripes
Shorts – Black
Telephone Nº: (0141) 955-9048
Ticket Office: (0141) 955-9048
Fax Number: (0141) 955-9049
Ground Capacity: 14,267
Seating Capacity: 5,257

SINCLAIR STREET

COWSHED · GRANDSTAND

EAST HAMILTON TERRACE
(DUBLIN END)

Clydebank are groundsharing with Greenock Morton during 2000/2001

GENERAL INFORMATION
Supporters Club: c/o Club
Telephone Nº: –
Car Parking: At the ground
Coach Parking: James Watt Dock
Nearest Railway Station: Cartsdyke (½ mile)
Nearest Bus Station: Town Centre (1½ miles)
Club Shop: c/o Office Address
Opening Times: Office Hours
Telephone Nº: (0141) 955-9048
Postal Sales: Yes
Nearest Police Station: Rue End Street, Greenock
Police Telephone Nº: (01475) 724444

GROUND INFORMATION
Away Supporters' Entrances & Sections:
East Hamilton Street turnstiles

ADMISSION INFO (2000/2001 PRICES)
Adult Standing: £8.00
Adult Seating: £10.00
Child Standing: £5.00
Child Seating: £5.00
Programme Price: £1.00

DISABLED INFORMATION
Wheelchairs: 5 spaces each for home and away fans
accommodated below the Grandstand
Helpers: Please phone the club for information
Prices: Please phone the club for information
Disabled Toilets: None
Are Bookings Necessary: Yes
Contact: (01475) 723571

Travelling Supporters' Information:
Routes: From All Parts: Take the M8 to the A8. Pass through Port Glasgow and turn left after passing the dock-
yard buildings on the right-hand side of the road.

COWDENBEATH FC

<table>
<tr><td>

Founded: 1881 (**Entered League:** 1921)
Former Names: The Miners FC
Nickname: 'Cowden' or 'Blue Brazil'
Ground: Central Park, High Street,
Cowdenbeath   KY4 9EY
Record Attendance: 25,586 (21/4/49)
Pitch Size: 107 × 64 yards

</td><td>

Colours: Shirts – Royal blue + white shoulders
Shorts – White with blue side panel
Telephone Nº: (01383) 610166
Ticket Office: (01383) 610166
Fax Number: (01383) 512132
Ground Capacity: 4,370
Seating Capacity: 1,431

</td></tr>
</table>

GENERAL INFORMATION

Supporters Club: W. Nellies, c/o Club
Telephone Nº: (01383) 610166
Car Parking: Car Park at the ground and Stenhouse Street (200 yards). A total of 200 spaces are available
Coach Parking: King Street and Rowan Terrace
Nearest Railway Station: Cowdenbeath (400 yards)
Nearest Bus Station: Cowdenbeath (Bus Stop at the ground)
Club Shop: At ground
Opening Times: Weekdays 10.00am to 3.00pm; Saturdays 1.00pm to 3.00pm
Telephone Nº: (01383) 610166
Postal Sales: Yes
Nearest Police Station: Cowdenbeath (300 yards)
Police Telephone Nº: (01383) 318600

GROUND INFORMATION

Away Supporters' Entrances & Sections:
Main Entrance for the South and East Sides

ADMISSION INFO (2000/2001 PRICES)

Adult Standing: £7.00
Adult Seating: £8.00
Child Standing: £3.00
Child Seating: £3.50
Programme Price: £1.00

DISABLED INFORMATION

Wheelchairs: 3 spaces each for home and away fans
Helpers: Please phone the club for information
Prices: Please phone the club for information
Disabled Toilets: 1 Ladies, 1 Gents and 1 Unisex available
Are Bookings Necessary: Yes
Contact: (01383) 610166

Travelling Supporters' Information:
Routes: Exit the M90 at Junction 3 for Dunfermline. Take the Dual Carriageway to Cowdenbeath and follow straight on into the High Street. The ground is situated on the first left turn in the High Street.

DUMBARTON FC

Founded: 1872 **(Entered League:** 1890)
Former Names: None
Nickname: 'Sons'
Ground: Until November 2000: Clifton Hill
Stadium, Main Street, Coatbridge ML5 3RB
Pitch Size: 110 × 72 yards

Colours: Shirts – Gold with Black Trim
Shorts – Black
Telephone Nº: (01389) 762569
Ticket Office: (01389) 762569
Fax Number: (01389) 762629
Ground Capacity: 2,496
Seating Capacity: 538

WEST END

MAIN STREET GRANDSTAND (Away)

ALBION STREET

CAR PARK

EAST END

Disabled Area

The club are groundsharing with Albion Rovers until November 2000

GENERAL INFORMATION
Supporters Club: c/o Club
Telephone Nº: –
Car Parking: Street Parking and Albion Street
Coach Parking: Albion Street
Nearest Railway Station: Coatdyke (10 mins. walk)
Nearest Bus Station: Coatbridge
Club Shop: None
Opening Times: –
Telephone Nº: –
Postal Sales: Yes
Nearest Police Station: Coatbridge (½ mile)
Police Telephone Nº: (01236) 50200

GROUND INFORMATION
Away Supporters' Entrances & Sections:
Main Street entrance for the Main Street Area

ADMISSION INFO (2000/2001 PRICES)
Adult Standing: £7.00
Adult Seating: £10.00
Child Standing: £3.50
Child Seating: £6.00
Programme Price: £1.00

DISABLED INFORMATION
Wheelchairs: Approximately 30 spaces available in the Disabled Area
Helpers: Please phone the club for information
Prices: Please phone the club for information
Disabled Toilets: One available at the East End of the Ground
Are Bookings Necessary: Yes
Contact: (01236) 606334

Dumbarton FC will be moving to a new ground near Dumbarton Castle in November 2000.

Travelling Supporters' Information:
Routes: From East or West: Take the A8/M8 to the Shawhead Interchange then follow the A725 to the Town Centre. Take A89 signs towards Airdrie at the roundabout, the ground is then on the left; From the South: Take the A725 from Bellshill/Hamilton/Motherwell/M74 to Coatbridge. Take A89 signs towards Airdrie at the roundabout, the ground is then on the left; From North: Take A73 to Airdrie then follow signs for A8010 to Coatbridge. Join the A89 and the ground is one mile on the right.

DUNDEE FC

Founded: 1893 (**Entered League:** 1893)
Former Names: None
Nickname: 'The Dark Blues'
Ground: Dens Park Stadium, Sandeman Street, Dundee DD3 7JY
Record Attendance: 43,024 (7/2/53)
Pitch Size: 105 × 68 yards

Colours: Shirts – Blue
Shorts – White
Telephone N°: (01382) 889966
Ticket Office: (01382) 204777
Fax Number: (01382) 832284
Ground Capacity: 12,054 (All seats)

WEST STAND

(DENS ROAD)
SOUTH ENCLOSURE

EAST STAND

SANDEMAN STREET CENTRE STAND (FAMILY SECTION)

TANNADICE STREET

GENERAL INFORMATION
Supporters Club: Dave Forbes, c/o Club
Telephone N°: (01382) 889966
Car Parking: Private 600 space Car Park available
Coach Parking: 50 yards from the ground
Nearest Railway Station: Dundee
Nearest Bus Station: Dundee
Club Shop: Commercial Street, Dundee
Opening Times: Weekdays 9.00am to 5.30pm
Telephone N°: (01382) 205664
Postal Sales: Yes
Nearest Police Station: Bell Street, Dundee
Police Telephone N°: (01382) 223200
GROUND INFORMATION
Away Supporters' Entrances & Sections:
Turnstiles 33-38 for East Stand and turnstiles 31-32 for Sections A, B & C of the Main Stand

ADMISSION INFO (2000/2001 PRICES)
Adult Seating: £13.00 – £16.00
Child Seating: £7.00 – £9.00
Note: Other reduced prices for children are available in the Family Stand
Programme Price: £1.50
DISABLED INFORMATION
Wheelchairs: Accommodated in the East and West Stands
Helpers: Admitted
Prices: Free for the disabled. Helpers £13.00
Disabled Toilets: Adjacent to the Disabled Area
Are Bookings Necessary: Yes
Contact: (01382) 826104

Web site: www.dundeefc.co.uk

Travelling Supporters' Information:
Routes: Take the A972 from Perth (Kingsway West) to King's Cross Circus Roundabout. Take the 3rd exit into Clepington Road and turn right into Provost Road for 1 mile then take the 2nd left into Sandeman Street for the ground.

DUNDEE UNITED FC

Founded: 1909 (**Entered League:** 1910)
Former Names: Dundee Hibernians FC
Nickname: 'The Terrors'
Ground: Tannadice Park, Tannadice Street, Dundee DD3 7JW
Record Attendance: 28,000 (Nov. 1996)
Pitch Size: 110 × 72 yards

Colours: Shirts – Tangerine
Shorts – Black
Telephone Nº: (01382) 833166
Ticket Office: (01382) 833166
Fax Number: (01382) 889398
Ground Capacity: 14,209 (all seats)

WEST STAND
(TANNADICE STREET)
FAIR PLAY STAND
SOUTH STAND
GEORGE FOX STAND
EAST STAND
ARKLAY STREET

GENERAL INFORMATION

Supporters Club: Andrew Woodrow, 3 Stevenson Avenue, Glenrothes KY6 1EE
Telephone Nº: (01592) 752129
Car Parking: Street Parking and Melrose Car Park
Coach Parking: Gussie Park (100 yards) and Dens Field
Nearest Railway Station: Dundee (20 mins. walk)
Nearest Bus Station: Dundee
Club Shop: At ground on Matchdays only or at 5 Victoria Road, Dundee
Opening Times: At ground: Matchdays 2.00pm to 5.00pm; Victoria Road: 9.00am to 5.30pm
Telephone Nº: (01382) 833166
Postal Sales: Yes
Nearest Police Station: Bell Street, Dundee
Police Telephone Nº: (01382) 223200

GROUND INFORMATION

Away Supporters' Entrances & Sections:
Turnstiles 7-16 for South Stand & Fair Play Stand

ADMISSION INFO (2000/2001 PRICES)

Adult Seating: £13.00 – £17.00
Child Seating: £8.00 – £10.00
Note: No concessions available on certain games
Programme Price: £1.50

DISABLED INFORMATION

Wheelchairs: Accommodated in the George Fox Stand and the East and West Stands
Helpers: Please phone the club for details
Prices: Please phone the club for details
Disabled Toilets: Available in the George Fox Stand and in the East and West Stands
Are Bookings Necessary: Yes
Contact: (01382) 833166

Travelling Supporters' Information:
Routes: From the South or West: Travel via Perth and take the A90 to Dundee. Once in Dundee join the Kingsway (ring road) and follow this road until the third roundabout then turn right onto Old Glamis Road. Follow the road to join Provost Road then turn left into Sandeman Street for the ground; From the North: Follow the A90 from Aberdeen and join the Kingsway (ring road). At the first set of traffic lights turn right into Clepington Road and follow into Arklay Street before turning left into Tannadice Street for the ground.

DUNFERMLINE ATHLETIC FC

Founded: 1885 (**Entered League:** 1921)
Former Names: None
Nickname: 'The Pars'
Ground: East End Park, Halbeath Road,
Dunfermline, Fife   KY12 7RB
Record Attendance: 27,816 (30/4/68)
Pitch Size: 115 × 70 yards

Colours: Shirts – Black & White Stripes
Shorts – Black
Telephone Nº: (01383) 724295
Ticket Office: (01383) 724295
Fax Number: (01383) 723468
Ground Capacity: 12,558 (All seats)

THE NORRIE
McCATHIE STAND

SOUTH MAIN STAND

WEST STAND

NORTH STAND

NORTH EAST STAND (Away)

(Away)
EAST STAND

GENERAL INFORMATION

Supporters Club: Mrs. J. Malcolm, 15 Meadowfield, Cowdenbeath
Telephone Nº: (01383) 611793
Car Parking: Street Parking and a Car Park at the ground. A Multistorey Car Park is 10 minutes walk
Coach Parking: Leys Park Road
Nearest Railway Station: Dunfermline (15 minutes walk)
Nearest Bus Station: Carnegie Drive, Dunfermline (10 minutes walk)
Club Shop: At the ground
Opening Times: Monday-Saturday 9.00am-5.30pm
Telephone Nº: (01383) 626737
Postal Sales: Yes
Nearest Police Station: Holyrood Place (10 minutes walk)
Police Telephone Nº: (01383) 726711

GROUND INFORMATION

Away Supporters' Entrances & Sections:
Turnstiles 10-15 for the East Stand. Turnstiles 16-18 for the North East Stand

ADMISSION INFO (2000/2001 PRICES)

Adult Seating: £10.00 – £19.00
Child Seating: £5.00 – £12.00
Note: Match prices vary according to the category of the game
Programme Price: £2.00

DISABLED INFORMATION

Wheelchairs: 12 spaces each for home & away fans
Helpers: One admitted per wheelchair
Prices: Free of charge for each wheelchair disabled and helper
Disabled Toilets: Available in West and East Stands
Are Bookings Necessary: Yes
Contact: (01383) 724295

Travelling Supporters' Information:
Routes: From the Forth Road Bridge and Perth: Exit the M90 at Junction 3 and take A907 (Halbeath Road) into Dunfermline – Ground on right;   From Kincardine Bridge and Alloa: Take A985 to A994 then into Dunfermline. Take Pittencrief Street, Glen Bridge and Carnegie Drive to Sinclair Gardens roundabout. Take 1st exit toward the Traffic Lights then turn right into Ley's Park Road. Take the second exit on the right into the Car Park at the rear of the stadium.

EAST FIFE FC

Founded: 1903 (**Entered League:** 1903)
Former Names: None
Nickname: 'The Fifers'
Ground: Bayview Stadium, Harbour
View, Methil, Fife KY8 3RW
Record Attendance: 22,515 (2/1/50)
Pitch Size: 113 × 73 yards

Colours: Shirts – Amber & Black Diamonds
Shorts – Black + Amber Stripes
Telephone Nº: (01333) 426323
Ticket Office: (01333) 426323
Fax Number: (01333) 426376
Ground Capacity: 2,000 (All seats)

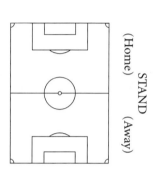

GENERAL INFORMATION
Supporters Club: Levenworth Supporters Club
Telephone Nº: (01592) 757249
Car Parking: Adjacent to the ground
Coach Parking: Adjacent to the ground
Nearest Railway Station: Kirkcaldy (8 miles)
Nearest Bus Station: Leven
Club Shop: At ground
Opening Times: Matchdays + normal office hours
Telephone Nº: (01333) 426323
Postal Sales: Yes
Nearest Police Station: Sea Road, Methil (1 mile)
Police Telephone Nº: (01592) 418900

GROUND INFORMATION
Away Supporters' Entrances & Sections:
Accommodated within the Main Stand

ADMISSION INFO (2000/2001 PRICES)
Adult Seating: £8.00
Child Seating: £4.00
Programme Price: £1.00

DISABLED INFORMATION
Wheelchairs: 24 spaces available in total
Helpers: Admitted
Prices: Normal prices charged
Disabled Toilets: Yes
Are Bookings Necessary: Yes
Contact: (01333) 426323

Travelling Supporters' Information:
Routes: Take the A915 from Kirkcaldy past Buckhaven and Methil to Leven. Turn right at traffic lights and go straight on at the first roundabout then turn right at the second roundabout. Cross Bawbee Bridge and turn left at the next roundabout. The ground is the first turning on the left after ¼ mile.

EAST STIRLINGSHIRE FC

Founded: 1881 (**Entered League:** 1900)
Former Names: Bainsford Britannia FC
Nickname: 'The Shire'
Ground: Firs Park, Firs Street, Falkirk
FK2 7AY
Record Attendance: 12,000 (21/2/21)
Pitch Size: 112 × 72 yards

Colours: Shirts – Black & White Hoops
Shorts – Black
Telephone Nº: (01324) 623583
Ticket Office: (01324) 623583
Fax Number: (01324) 637862
Ground Capacity: 780
Seating Capacity: 280

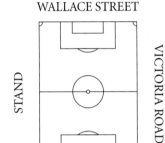

WALLACE STREET

STAND

VICTORIA ROAD

GENERAL INFORMATION
Supporters Club: None
Telephone Nº: –
Car Parking: Street Parking
Coach Parking: Street Parking
Nearest Railway Station: Grahamston (10 minutes walk)
Nearest Bus Station: Falkirk
Club Shop: At ground
Opening Times: Weekdays (except Thursdays) and Saturday Matchdays 10.00am to 2.30pm
Telephone Nº: (01324) 623583
Postal Sales: Yes
Nearest Police Station: Falkirk (½ mile)
Police Telephone Nº: (01324) 634212

GROUND INFORMATION
Away Supporters' Entrances & Sections:
No usual segregation

ADMISSION INFO (2000/2001 PRICES)
Adult Standing: £6.00
Adult Seating: £7.00
OAP and Child Standing: £3.00
OAP and Child Seating: £3.00
Programme Price: £1.00

DISABLED INFORMATION
Wheelchairs: Accommodated
Helpers: Admitted
Prices: £3.00 each for both disabled and helpers
Disabled Toilets: Available in the Main Stand
Are Bookings Necessary: Yes
Contact: (01324) 623583

Travelling Supporters' Information:
Routes: From Glasgow and Edinburgh: Exit the Motorway at signs marked Grangemouth. Follow the AA signs for football traffic into Falkirk as far as Thornhill Road (where the road meets the 'Give Way' sign). Once in Thornhill Road turn left into Firs Street at St. James' Church. The Ground is straight ahead.

ELGIN CITY FC

Founded: 1893
Former Names: None
Nickname: 'Black and Whites'
Ground: Borough Briggs, Borough Briggs Road, Elgin   IV30 1AP
Record Attendance: 12,640 (17/2/68)
Pitch Size: 120 × 86 yards
Colours: Shirts – Black and White
Shorts – Black and Red

Telephone Nº: (01343) 547921
Ticket Information: (01343) 551114
Fax Number: (01343) 814133
Ground Capacity: 8,000
Seating Capacity: 450
Contact Address: J. Meichan, 30 Reidhaven Street, Elgin
Contact Phone Nº: (01343) 550850
Contact Fax Nº: (01343) 547921

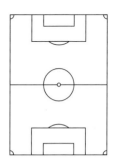

GENERAL INFORMATION

Supporters Club: Mrs. C. Jack, c/o Club
Telephone Nº: (01343) 545196
Car Parking: At the ground
Coach Parking: At the ground
Nearest Railway Station: Elgin (1 mile)
Nearest Bus Station: Elgin (¼ mile)
Club Shop: At the ground
Opening Times: Weekdays 8.30am to 5.30pm and also Saturdays 8.30am to 3.00pm
Telephone Nº: (01343) 551114
Postal Sales: Yes
Nearest Police Station: Elgin (1 mile)
Police Telephone Nº: (01343) 543101

GROUND INFORMATION

Away Supporters' Entrances & Sections:
West End entrances for the Covered Enclosure

ADMISSION INFO (2000/2001 PRICES)

Adult Standing: £6.00
Adult Seating: £7.00
Child Standing: £2.00
Child Seating: £3.00
Programme Price: £1.00

DISABLED INFORMATION

Wheelchairs: Accommodated
Helpers: Admitted
Prices: Disabled admitted at concessionary prices
Disabled Toilets: Yes
Are Bookings Necessary: No
Contact: (01343) 550850 (J. Meichan, Secretary)

Travelling Supporters' Information:
Routes: Take the Alexandra bypass to the roundabout ½ mile from the City Centre and turn left towards Lossiemouth. Borough Briggs Road is on the left.

FALKIRK FC

Founded: 1876 (**Entered League:** 1902)
Former Names: None
Nickname: 'The Bairns'
Ground: Brockville Park, Hope Street, Falkirk FK1 5AX
Record Attendance: 23,100 (21/2/53)
Pitch Size: 110 × 70 yards

Colours: Shirts – Navy Blue
Shorts – White
Telephone Nº: (01324) 624121
Ticket Office: (01324) 624121
Fax Number: (01324) 612418
Ground Capacity: 7,576
Seating Capacity: 1,700

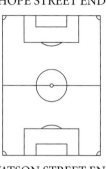

HOPE STREET END

COVERED ENCLOSURE
DISABLED ENCLOSURE

STAND   CAR PARK

WATSON STREET END

GENERAL INFORMATION

Supporters Club: Gordon McFarlane, 1 Summerford Gardens, Falkirk
Telephone Nº: (01324) 638104
Car Parking: Car Park at ground (200 spaces) and also Town Car Park
Coach Parking: Town Car Park (100 yards)
Nearest Railway Station: Grahamston (100 yards)
Nearest Bus Station: Falkirk Centre (800 yards)
Club Shop: Glebe Street, Falkirk
Opening Times: 9.00am to 5.00pm
Telephone Nº: (01324) 639366
Postal Sales: Yes
Nearest Police Station: Hope Street, Falkirk (½ mile)
Police Telephone Nº: (01324) 634212

GROUND INFORMATION

Away Supporters' Entrances & Sections:
Watson Street entrances for the Watson Street End

ADMISSION INFO (2000/2001 PRICES)

Adult Standing: £10.00 – £11.50
Adult Seating: £13.50 – £15.00
Child Standing: £5.00 (£2.00 for Under-11's)
Child Seating: £6.50
Programme Price: £1.50

DISABLED INFORMATION

Wheelchairs: 14 spaces by the Watson Street Side
Helpers: Admitted
Prices: Normal prices charged
Disabled Toilets: Yes
Are Bookings Necessary: Yes
Contact: (01324) 624121

Travelling Supporters' Information:
Routes: From North and West: Exit M876 Junction 1 and take A883 into A803 to Falkirk. Pass along Camelon Road and West Bridge Street and turn left into Hope Street by Police Station. Follow along over railway line for Ground (about half a mile); From South & East: Take A803 road from Linlithglow into Falkirk along Callendar Road. Pass Callendar Shopping Centre (on right) along High Street and turn right into Hope Street by the Drookit & Duck pub (then as North & West).

FORFAR ATHLETIC FC

Founded: 1885 (**Entered League:** 1921)
Former Names: None
Nickname: 'Loons'
Ground: Station Park, Carseview Road, Forfar, Tayside
Record Attendance: 10,780 (2/2/70)
Pitch Size: 115 × 69 yards

Colours: Shirts – Sky Blue + Navy Trim
Shorts – Navy Blue
Telephone Nº: (01307) 463576
Ticket Office: (01307) 463576
Fax Number: (01307) 466956
Ground Capacity: 8,388
Seating Capacity: 739

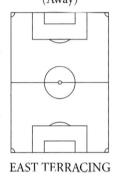

WEST END TERRACING
(Away)

SOUTH TERRACING (COVERED)

NORTH – MAIN STAND

EAST TERRACING

GENERAL INFORMATION

Supporters Club: Mrs. Y. Nicoll, 24 Turfbeg Drive, Forfar DD8 3LH
Telephone Nº: (01307) 467255
Car Parking: Market Muir Car Park and adjacent streets
Coach Parking: Mark Muir Car Park
Nearest Railway Station: Dundee or Arbroath (both 14 miles)
Nearest Bus Station: Forfar (½ mile)
Club Shop: None
Opening Times: –
Telephone Nº: –
Postal Sales: Yes
Nearest Police Station: West High Street, Forfar
Police Telephone Nº: (01307) 462551

GROUND INFORMATION

Away Supporters' Entrances & Sections:
West End entrances for West End Terracing and North part of the Main Stand

ADMISSION INFO (2000/2001 PRICES)

Adult Standing: £7.00
Adult Seating: £7.50
Child Standing: £3.00
Child Seating: £3.50
Programme Price: £1.00

DISABLED INFORMATION

Wheelchairs: 4 spaces each for home and away fans accommodated to the west of the Main Stand
Helpers: Please phone the club for details
Prices: Please phone the club for details
Disabled Toilets: One available
Are Bookings Necessary: Yes
Contact: (01307) 463576

Travelling Supporters' Information:
Routes: Take A85/M90 to Dundee and then the A929. Exit at the 2nd turn-off (signposted Forfar). On the outskirts of Forfar, turn right at the T-junction and then left at the next major road. The ground is signposted on the left (cobbled street with railway arch).

GREENOCK MORTON FC

Founded: 1874 (**Entered League:** 1893)
Former Names: None
Nickname: 'Ton'
Ground: Cappielow Park, Sinclair Street,
Greenock   PA15 2TY
Record Attendance: 23,500 (29/4/21)
Pitch Size: 110 × 71 yards

Colours: Shirts – Blue and White Hoops
Shorts – White
Telephone Nº: (01475) 723571
Ticket Office: (01475) 723571
Fax Number: (01475) 781084
Ground Capacity: 14,267
Seating Capacity: 5,257

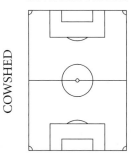

SINCLAIR STREET

COWSHED

GRANDSTAND

EAST HAMILTON TERRACE
(DUBLIN END)

GENERAL INFORMATION
Supporters Club Liaison: Gary W. Miller, c/o Club
Telephone Nº: (01475) 888812
Car Parking: At the ground
Coach Parking: James Watt Dock
Nearest Railway Station: Cartsdyke (½ mile)
Nearest Bus Station: Town Centre (1½ miles)
Club Shop: The Morton Club Shop, 85 Cathcart
Street, Greenock PA15 1DE
Opening Times: Weekdays 9.00am to 5.00pm.
Saturdays 10.00am to 3.00pm
Telephone Nº: (01475) 785855/888812
Postal Sales: Yes
Nearest Police Station: Rue End Street, Greenock
Police Telephone Nº: (01475) 724444

GROUND INFORMATION
Away Supporters' Entrances & Sections:
East Hamilton Street turnstiles

ADMISSION INFO (2000/2001 PRICES)
Adult Standing: £10.00
Adult Seating: £11.00
Child Standing: £6.00
Child Seating: £5.00
Programme Price: £1.50

DISABLED INFORMATION
Wheelchairs: 5 spaces each for home and away fans
accommodated below the Grandstand
Helpers: One helper admitted per disabled fan
Prices: Free of charge for the disabled and helpers
Disabled Toilets: None
Are Bookings Necessary: Yes
Contact: (01475) 723571

Web site: www.greenockmorton.co.uk

Travelling Supporters' Information:
Routes: From All Parts: Take the M8 to the A8. Pass through Port Glasgow and turn left after passing the dock-
yard buildings on the right-hand side of the road.

HAMILTON ACADEMICAL FC

Founded: 1874 (**Entered League:** 1897)
Former Names: None
Nickname: 'The Accies'
Ground: Firhill Stadium, 80 Firhill Road, Glasgow G20 7AL
Record Attendance: 49,838 (18/2/22)
Note: The club is currently groundsharing with Partick Thistle FC

Colours: Shirts – Red and White Hoops
Shorts – White with Red Flash
Telephone N°: (01698) 286103
Fax Number: (01698) 285422
Correspondence Address: Enable Building, Prospect House, New Park Street, Hamilton ML3 0BN
Pitch Size: 111 × 76 yards
Ground Capacity: 14,538 (9,076 seats)

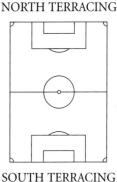

NORTH TERRACING

MAIN STAND
FIRHILL ROAD

JACKIE HUSBAND STAND

SOUTH TERRACING

GENERAL INFORMATION

Supporters Club: J. Galloway, c/o Club
Telephone N°: –
Car Parking: Street parking
Coach Parking: By Police Direction
Nearest Railway Station: Glasgow Queen Street/ Glasgow Central/Maryhill
Nearest Underground Station: St. George's Cross/ Kelvinbridge
Club Shop: Contact the Club Office
Opening Times: Office Hours
Telephone N°: (01698) 286103
Postal Sales: Yes
Nearest Police Station: Maryhill
Police Telephone N°: (0141) 532-3700

GROUND INFORMATION

Away Supporters' Entrances & Sections:
All spectators will enter via the Jackie Husband Stand turnstiles

ADMISSION INFO (2000/2001 PRICES)

Adult Seating: £10.00
Child/Senior Citizen Seating: £5.00
Programme Price: £1.00

DISABLED INFORMATION

Wheelchairs: 17 spaces in the North Enclosure
Helpers: Admitted following advance notification
Prices: Free for the disabled and one helper
Disabled Toilets: One available in the Main Stand
Are Bookings Necessary: Yes
Contact: (01698) 286103

Travelling Supporters' Information:
Routes: From the East: Leave the M8 at Junction 16; From the West: Leave the M8 at Junction 17. From both, follow Maryhill Road to Queen's Cross and the ground is on the right.

HEART OF MIDLOTHIAN FC

Founded: 1874 (**Entered League:** 1890)
Former Names: None
Nickname: 'The Jam Tarts' & 'Jambo's'
Ground: Tynecastle Stadium, Gorgie
Road, Edinburgh   EH11 2NL
Record Attendance: 53,496 (13/1/32)
Pitch Size: 107 × 73 yards

Colours: Shirts – Maroon
   Shorts – White
Telephone Nº: (0131) 200-7200
Ticket Office: (0131) 200-7201
Fax Number: (0131) 200-7222
Ground Capacity: 18,000 (All seats)

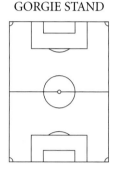

GORGIE STAND

McLEOD STREET MAIN STAND

WHEATFIELD STAND

ROSEBURN STAND

GENERAL INFORMATION

Supporters Club: J.N. Borthwick, 21/9 Festival
Gardens, Edinburgh   EH11 1RB
Telephone Nº: (0131) 313-4924
Car Parking: Street Parking in Robertson Avenue
and Westfield Road
Coach Parking: Russell Road
Nearest Railway Station: Edinburgh Haymarket
(½ mile)
Nearest Bus Station: St. Andrew's Square
Club Superstore: Gorgie Stand/Tynecastle Terrace
Opening Times: Weekdays 9.30am to 5.30pm and
Matchdays 9.30am to 5.00pm
Telephone Nº: (0131) 200-7211
Postal Sales: Yes
Nearest Police Station: Haymarket, Edinburgh
Police Telephone Nº: (0131) 229-2323

GROUND INFORMATION

Away Supporters' Entrances & Sections:
Roseburn Stand entrances and accommodation

ADMISSION INFO (2000/2001 PRICES)

Adult Seating: £16.00 – £19.00
Child Seating: £8 or £10 (In the Family Area only)
Adult Seating: £16.00 – £19.00
Note: Prices vary according to the category of game

DISABLED INFORMATION

Wheelchairs: 100 spaces available for home and
away fans in Wheatfield, Roseburn & Gorgie Stands
Helpers: Admitted
Prices: Please contact the club for details
Disabled Toilets: Available
Are Bookings Necessary: Yes
Contact: (0131) 200-7222

Web site: www.heartsfc.co.uk

Travelling Supporters' Information:
Routes: From West: Take A71 (Ayr Road) into Gorgie Road, ground is about ¾ mile past Saughton Park on left;
From North: Take A90 Queensferry Road and turn right into Drum Brae in about ½ mile. Follow Drum Brae
into Meadowplace Road (about 1 mile) then Broomhouse Road to junction with Calder Road. Turn right then as
from West; From South: Take A702/A703 to A720 (Oxgangs Road). Turn left and follow A720 into Wester Hailes
Road (2½ miles) until the junction with Calder Road. Turn right – then as from West.

HIBERNIAN FC

Founded: 1875 (**Entered League:** 1893)
Former Names: None
Nickname: 'The Hi-Bees'
Ground: Easter Road Stadium, Albion Road, Edinburgh EH7 5QG
Record Attendance: 65,840 (2/1/50)
Pitch Size: 112 × 74 yards

Colours: Shirts – Green and White
Shorts – White
Telephone Nº: (0131) 661-2159
Ticket Office: (0131) 661-1875
Fax Number: (0131) 659-6488
Ground Capacity: 16,032 (All seats)

ALBION PLACE
THE FAMOUS FIVE STAND

WEST STAND (North) (Centre) (South)

EAST SEATED TERRACE

SOUTH STAND LOWER (Away)
SOUTH STAND UPPER (Home)
ALBION ROAD

GENERAL INFORMATION

Supporters Club: W. Alcorn, 11 Sunnyside, Easter Road Lane, Edinburgh
Telephone Nº: (0131) 661-3157
Car Parking: Street Parking
Coach Parking: By Police Direction
Nearest Railway Station: Edinburgh Waverley (25 minutes walk)
Nearest Bus Station: St. Andrew's Square
Club Shop: North Stand
Opening Times: Tuesday-Friday 9.00am to 5.00pm, Matchdays 9.00am to kick-off
Telephone Nº: (0131) 656-7078
Postal Sales: Yes
Nearest Police Station: Queen Charlotte St., Leith
Police Telephone Nº: (0131) 554-9350

GROUND INFORMATION

Away Supporters' Entrances & Sections:
South Stand (Lower) entrances and accommodation

ADMISSION INFO (2000/2001 PRICES)

Adult Seating: £15.00 – £21.00
Child Seating: £10.00
Programme Price: £2.00

DISABLED INFORMATION

Wheelchairs: 30 spaces in total in the South Seated Enclosure and the Famous Five and South Stands
Helpers: One helper admitted per wheelchair
Prices: Free for the disabled. Helpers £21.00
Disabled Toilets: 2 available in the North and South Stands
Are Bookings Necessary: Yes
Contact: (0131) 661-2159

Web site: www.hibernianfc.co.uk

Travelling Supporters' Information:
Routes: From West & North: Take A90 Queensferry Road to A902 and continue for 2¼ miles. Turn right into Great Junction Street and follow into Duke Street then Lochend Road. Turn sharp right into Hawkhill Avenue at Lochend Park and follow road into Albion Place for Ground; From South: Take A1 through Musselburgh (Milton Road/Willow Brae/London Road) and turn right into Easter Road after about 2½ miles. Take 4th right into Albion Road for Ground.

INVERNESS CALEDONIAN THISTLE FC

Founded: 1994 (**Entered League:** 1994)
Former Names: Caledonian Thistle FC
Nickname: 'The Jags' 'Caley'
Ground: Caledonian Stadium, East Longman, Inverness IV1 1FF
Record Attendance: 9,370 (Telford Street) (1/3/58)
Colours: Shirts – Royal blue/white + red panels
Shorts – White

Telephone Nº: (01463) 222880 (Ground)
Ticket Office: (01463) 222880
Fax Number: (01463) 715816
Pitch Size: 115 × 80 yards
Ground Capacity: 6,000
Seating Capacity: 2,000 (approximately)
Contact Address: Mr. J. Falconer, 17 Culloden Park, Inverness
Contact Phone Nº: (01463) 792358

  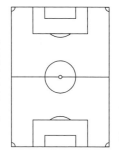

GENERAL INFORMATION
Supporters Club: c/o Club
Telephone Nº: (01463) 222880
Car Parking: At the ground
Coach Parking: At the ground
Nearest Railway Station: Inverness (1 mile)
Nearest Bus Station: Inverness
Club Shop: At the ground
Opening Times: Monday to Friday and Matchdays 9.00am – 5.00pm
Telephone Nº: (01463) 222880
Postal Sales: Yes
Nearest Police Station: Longman Road, Inverness
Police Telephone Nº: (01463) 704006

GROUND INFORMATION
Away Supporters' Entrances & Sections:
Accommodation on the East Side of the Main Stand

ADMISSION INFO (2000/2001 PRICES)
Adult Standing: £9.00
Adult Seating: £11.00
Child Standing: £3.00
Child Seating: £6.00
Programme Price: £1.50

DISABLED INFORMATION
Wheelchairs: 16 spaces available in total
Helpers: Please phone the club for details
Prices: Please phone the club for details
Disabled Toilets: Yes
Are Bookings Necessary: Yes
Contact: (01463) 222880

Travelling Supporters' Information:
Routes: The ground is adjacent to Kessock Bridge. From the South: Take the A9 to Inverness and turn right at the roundabout before the bridge over the Moray Firth; From the North: Take the A9 over the bridge and turn left at the roundabout for the ground.

KILMARNOCK FC

Founded: 1869 (**Entered League:** 1896)
Former Names: None
Nickname: 'Killie'
Ground: Rugby Park, Rugby Road, Kilmarnock, Ayrshire KA1 2DP
Record Attendance: 34,246 (17/8/63)
Pitch Size: 115 × 74 yards

Colours: Shirts – Blue & White Stripes
    Shorts – White
Telephone Nº: (01563) 545300
Fax Number: (01563) 522181
Ground Capacity: 18,218 (all seats)

DUNDONALD ROAD END
MOFFAT STAND

EAST STAND

WEST STAND

CHADWICK STAND (Away)
(RUGBY ROAD END)

GENERAL INFORMATION

Supporters Club: c/o Club
Telephone Nº: (01563) 545317
Car Parking: At the ground (Permit Holders only)
Coach Parking: Fairyhill Road Bus Park
Nearest Railway Station: Kilmarnock (15 mins. walk)
Nearest Bus Station: Kilmarnock (10 mins. walk)
Club Shop: JJB Sports, Glencairn Square, Kilmarnock
Opening Times: Monday to Saturday 9.00am to 5.00pm
Telephone Nº: (01563) 545306
Postal Sales: Yes
Nearest Police Station: St. Marnock Street, Kilmarnock
Police Telephone Nº: (01563) 521188

GROUND INFORMATION

Away Supporters' Entrances & Sections:
Rugby Road turnstiles for the Chadwick Stand

ADMISSION INFO (2000/2001 PRICES)

Adult Seating: £13.00 – £16.00
Child Seating: £6.00 – £7.00
Programme Price: £1.50

DISABLED INFORMATION

Wheelchairs: 15 spaces each for home and away fans in the Main Stand
Helpers: One helper admitted per wheelchair
Prices: £3.00 for the disabled. Helpers £5.00
Disabled Toilets: 2 available in the Chadwick Stand and Moffat Stand
Are Bookings Necessary: Yes
Contact: (01292) 288905

Web site: www.kilmarnockfc.co.uk

Travelling Supporters' Information:
Routes: From Glasgow/Ayr: Take the A77 Kilmarnock Bypass. Exit at the Bellfield Interchange. Take the A71 (Irvine) to the first roundabout then take the A759 (Kilmarnock Town Centre). The ground is ½ mile on the left hand side.

LIVINGSTON FC

Founded: 1943 (**Entered League:** 1974)
Former Names: Ferranti Thistle FC,
Meadowbank Thistle FC
Nickname: 'The Lions'
Ground: Almondvale Stadium,
Alderstone Road, Livingston EH54 7DN
Record Attendance: 6,013 (1/4/99)

Colours: Shirts – Amber with Black trim
Shorts – Amber with Black trim
Telephone N°: (01506) 417000
Ticket Office: (01506) 417000
Fax Number: (01506) 418888
Pitch Size: 105 × 72 yards
Ground Capacity: 6,107 (All seats)

NORTH STAND
(Away)

WEST STAND

EAST STAND (Away)

SOUTH STAND

GENERAL INFORMATION

Supporters Club: Duncan Bennett, 63 Granby
Avenue, Howden, Livingston EH54 6LD
Telephone N°: (01506) 495113
Car Parking: Car Park at the ground
Coach Parking: At the ground
Nearest Railway Station: Livingston
Nearest Bus Station: Livingston
Club Shop: Beneath the West Stand
Opening Times: Matchdays and by request in the
week
Telephone N°: (01506) 417000
Postal Sales: Yes
Nearest Police Station: Livingston
Police Telephone N°: (01506) 431200

GROUND INFORMATION

Away Supporters' Entrances & Sections:
North Stand entrances and accommodation

ADMISSION INFO (2000/2001 PRICES)

Adult Seating: £10.00
Child Seating: £5.00
Programme Price: £1.50

DISABLED INFORMATION

Wheelchairs: Accommodated
Helpers: Please phone the club for information
Prices: Please phone the club for information
Disabled Toilets: Yes
Are Bookings Necessary: Yes
Contact: (01506) 417000

Web site: www.livingstonfc.co.uk

Travelling Supporters' Information:
Routes: Exit the M8 at the Livingston turn-off and take the A899 to the Cousland Interchange. Turn right into
Cousland Road, pass the Hospital, then turn left into Alderstone Road and the stadium is on the left opposite the
Campus.

MONTROSE FC

Founded: 1879 (**Entered League:** 1929)
Former Names: None
Nickname: 'Gable Endies'
Ground: Links Park Stadium, Wellington Street, Montrose DD10 8QD
Record Attendance: 8,983 (17/3/73)
Pitch Size: 113 × 70 yards

Colours: Shirts – Royal Blue & White stripes
  Shorts – Royal Blue
Telephone No: (01674) 673200
Ticket Office: (01674) 673200
Fax Number: (01674) 677311
Ground Capacity: 4,500
Seating Capacity: 1,338

GENERAL INFORMATION

Supporters Club: c/o Links Park
Telephone No: –
Car Parking: At the ground and Street Parking also
Coach Parking: Mid Links
Nearest Railway Station: Montrose Western Road
Nearest Bus Station: High Street, Montrose
Club Shop: At ground
Opening Times: Fridays and Matchdays 10.00am to 5.00pm
Telephone No: (01674) 673200
Postal Sales: Yes
Nearest Police Station: George Street, Montrose (15 minutes walk)
Police Telephone No: (01674) 672222

GROUND INFORMATION

Away Supporters' Entrances & Sections:
No usual segregation

ADMISSION INFO (2000/2001 PRICES)

Adult Standing: £7.00
Adult Seating: £7.50
Child Standing: £3.50
Child Seating: £4.00
Programme Price: £1.00

DISABLED INFORMATION

Wheelchairs: 5 spaces available in the Main Stand
Helpers: Please phone the club for information
Prices: Please phone the club for information
Disabled Toilets: 2 available in the Main Stand
Are Bookings Necessary: No, but they are helpful
Contact: (01674) 673200

Travelling Supporters' Information:
Routes: Take the main A92 Coastal Road to Montrose. Once in the town, the ground is well signposted and is situated in the Mid-Links area.

MOTHERWELL FC

Founded: 1886 (**Entered League:** 1893)
Former Names: None
Nickname: 'The Well'
Ground: Firpark, Firpark Street,
Motherwell ML1 2QN
Record Attendance: 35,632 (12/3/52)
Pitch Size: 110 × 75 yards

Colours: Shirts – Amber with claret hoop
Shorts – White
Telephone Nº: (01698) 333333
Ticket Office: (01698) 338006
Fax Number: (01698) 338001
Ground Capacity: 13,742

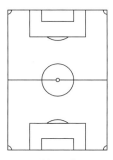

D. COOPER STAND

(FIRPARK STREET)
MAIN STAND

EAST STAND

(Away)
SOUTH STAND

GENERAL INFORMATION
Supporters Club: Jim Fleming, c/o Firpark
Telephone Nº: (01555) 759127
Car Parking: Street Parking and nearby Car Parks
Coach Parking: Orbiston Street
Nearest Railway Station: Motherwell (1½ miles)
Nearest Bus Station: Motherwell
Club Shop: At ground
Opening Times: Saturday Matchdays 10.00am to 3.00pm
Telephone Nº: (01698) 338025
Postal Sales: Yes
Nearest Police Station: Motherwell (¼ mile)
Police Telephone Nº: (01698) 483000

GROUND INFORMATION
Away Supporters' Entrances & Sections:
Dalziel Drive entrances for the South Stand

ADMISSION INFO (2000/2001 PRICES)
Adult Seating: £13.00 – £18.00
Child Seating: £7.00 – £9.00
Note: Discounts are available in the Family Section
Programme Price: £1.50

DISABLED INFORMATION
Wheelchairs: 12 spaces for home fans and 6 spaces for away fans in the South-West enclosure.
Helpers: Admitted
Prices: Please phone the club for information
Disabled Toilets: One available close to the Disabled Area
Are Bookings Necessary: Yes – 1 week in advance
Contact: (01698) 333333

Web site: www.motherwellfc.co.uk

Travelling Supporters' Information:
Routes: From the East: Take A723 into Merry Street and turn left into Brandon Street (1 mile). Follow through to Windmill Hill Street and turn right at Fire Station into Knowetop Avenue for Ground; From Elsewhere: Exit M74 Junction 4 and take A723 Hamilton Road into Town Centre. Turn right into West Hamilton Street and follow into Brandon Street – then as from the East.

PARTICK THISTLE FC

Founded: 1876 (**Entered League:** 1890)
Former Names: None
Nickname: 'The Jags'
Ground: Firhill Stadium, 80 Firhill Road, Glasgow G20 7AL
Record Attendance: 49,838 (18/2/22)
Pitch Size: 111 × 76 yards

Colours: Shirts – Red and Yellow Hoops
Shorts – White
Telephone Nº: (0141) 579-1971
Ticket Office: (0141) 579-1971
Fax Number: (0141) 945-1525
Ground Capacity: 14,538
Seating Capacity: 8,397

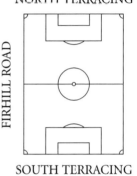

NORTH TERRACING

MAIN STAND
FIRHILL ROAD

JACKIE HUSBAND STAND

SOUTH TERRACING

GENERAL INFORMATION

Supporters Club: c/o Partick Thistle F.C., Firhill Stadium, Glasgow G20 7AL
Car Parking: Street Parking
Coach Parking: By Police Direction
Nearest Railway Station: Maryhill
Nearest Underground Station: St. George's Cross
Club Shops: At the Stadium
Opening Times: Matchdays 11.30am to 5.00pm or 5.00pm to 9.30pm for Night matches. Also Wednesdays 12.00pm to 4.00pm
Telephone Nº: (0141) 579-1971
Postal Sales: Yes
Nearest Police Station: Maryhill
Police Telephone Nº: (0141) 532-3700

GROUND INFORMATION

Away Supporters' Entrances & Sections:
At the North end of the Jackie Husband Stand

ADMISSION INFO (2000/2001 PRICES)

Adult Seating: £10.00
Senior Citizen/Child Seating: £5.00
Under 12's Seating: £3.00
Programme Price: £1.50

DISABLED INFORMATION

Wheelchairs: 17 spaces in the North Enclosure
Helpers: One helper admitted per wheelchair
Prices: Free for the disabled and one helper
Disabled Toilets: One available in the Main Stand
Are Bookings Necessary: Yes – contact the Club Secretary
Contact: (0141) 579-1971

Travelling Supporters' Information:
Routes: From the East: Leave the M8 at Junction 16; From the West: Leave the M8 at Junction 17. From both, follow Maryhill Road to Queen's Cross and the ground is on the right.

PETERHEAD FC

<table>
<tr><td>

Founded: 1891
Former Names: None
Nickname: 'Blue Toon'
Ground: Balmoor Stadium, Peterhead
AB42 6HG
Record Attendance: Not known
Colours: Shirts – Royal Blue + White Sleeves
Shorts – White

</td><td>

Telephone Nº: (01779) 478256
Fax Number: (01779) 475075
Ground Capacity: 4,000
Seating Capacity: 470
Pitch Size: 110 × 74 yards
Contact Address: G. Ritchie, 18 Skelton
Street, Peterhead
Contact Phone Nº: (01779) 473434

</td></tr>
</table>

STAND

GENERAL INFORMATION
Supporters Club: None
Telephone Nº: –
Car Parking: At the ground
Coach Parking: At the ground
Nearest Railway Station: Aberdeen
Nearest Bus Station: Peterhead
Club Shop: None
Opening Times: –
Telephone Nº: –
Postal Sales: –
Nearest Police Station: Peterhead
Police Telephone Nº: (01779) 472571

GROUND INFORMATION
Away Supporters' Entrances & Sections:
No usual segregation

ADMISSION INFO (2000/2001 PRICES)
Adult Standing: £6.00
Adult Seating: £7.50
Child Standing: £3.00
Child Seating: £4.00
Programme Price: £1.00

DISABLED INFORMATION
Wheelchairs: Accommodated
Helpers: Please phone the club for details
Prices: Please phone the club for details
Disabled Toilets: Yes
Are Bookings Necessary: Yes
Contact: (01779) 473434

Travelling Supporters' Information:
Routes: The ground is situated on the left of the main road from Fraserburgh (A952), about 300 yards past the swimming pool.

QUEEN OF THE SOUTH FC

Founded: 1919 (**Entered League:** 1923)	**Colours:** Shirts – Blue
Former Names: None	Shorts – Blue
Nickname: 'The Doonhamers'	**Telephone Nº:** (01387) 254853
Ground: Palmerston Park, Terregles	**Ticket Office:** (01387) 254853
Street, Dumfries DG2 9BA	**Fax Number:** (01387) 254853
Record Attendance: 24,500 (23/2/52)	**Ground Capacity:** 6,412
Pitch Size: 112 × 73 yards	**Seating Capacity:** 3,509

PORTLAND ROAD

WEST STAND

EAST STAND (Away)

(Away)
TERREGLES STREET END

GENERAL INFORMATION

Supporters Club: G. Corbett, 12 Loch Road, Dumfries
Telephone Nº: (01387) 262180
Car Parking: Car Park adjacent to the ground
Coach Parking: Car Park adjacent to the ground
Nearest Railway Station: Dumfries (¾ mile)
Nearest Bus Station: Dumfries Whitesands (5 minutes walk)
Club Shop: At ground
Opening Times: Daily
Telephone Nº: (01387) 254853
Postal Sales: Yes – Contact the Club
Nearest Police Station: Dumfries (½ mile)
Police Telephone Nº: (01387) 252112

GROUND INFORMATION

Away Supporters' Entrances & Sections:
Terregles Street entrances for the Terregles Street End and part of the East Stand

ADMISSION INFO (2000/2001 PRICES)

Adult Standing: £9.00
Adult Seating: £9.00
Child Standing: £3.00
Child Seating: £6.00
Programme Price: £1.20

DISABLED INFORMATION

Wheelchairs: Accommodated in front of the East Stand
Helpers: Please phone the club for details
Prices: Please phone the club for details
Disabled Toilets: One available in the East Stand
Are Bookings Necessary: Yes
Contact: (01387) 254853

Web site: www.qosfc.co.uk

Travelling Supporters' Information:
Routes: From East: Take the A75 to Dumfries and follow ring road over the River Nith. Turn left at 1st roundabout then right at 2nd roundabout (the Kilmarnock/Glasgow Road roundabout). Ground is a short way along adjacent to the Tesco store; From West: Take the A75 to Dumfries and proceed along ring road to 1st roundabout (Kilmarnock/Glasgow Road) then as East; From North: Take the A76 to Dumfries and carry straight across 1st roundabout for ground.

QUEEN'S PARK FC

Founded: 1867 (**Entered League:** 1900)
Former Names: None
Nickname: 'The Spiders'
Ground: Hampden Park, Mount Florida, Glasgow G42 9BA
Record Attendance: 150,239 (17/4/37)
Pitch Size: 115 × 75 yards

Colours: Shirts – Black and White Hoops
Shorts – White
Telephone Nº: (0141) 632-1275
Ticket Office: (0141) 632-1275
Fax Number: (0141) 636-1612
Ground Capacity: 52,000 (All seats)

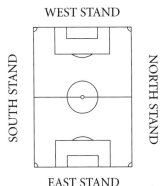

WEST STAND

SOUTH STAND

NORTH STAND

EAST STAND

GENERAL INFORMATION

Supporters Club: K. McAllister, 58 Brunton Street, Glasgow G44
Telephone Nº: (0141) 637-6075
Car Parking: Car Park at the Stadium
Coach Parking: Car Park at the Stadium
Nearest Railway Station: Mount Florida and King's Park (both 5 minutes walk)
Nearest Bus Station: Buchanan Street
Club Shop: At the ground
Opening Times: During home matches only
Telephone Nº: (0141) 632-1275
Postal Sales: Yes
Nearest Police Station: Aikenhead Road, Glasgow
Police Telephone Nº: (0141) 532-4900

Club Web site: www.queensparkfc.co.uk

GROUND INFORMATION

Away Supporters' Entrances & Sections:
South Stand

ADMISSION INFO (2000/2001 PRICES)

Adult Seating: £7.00 (Cup ties £8.00)
Child Seating: £2.00 (Cup ties £3.00)
Programme Price: £1.00
Note: Only the South Stand is presently in use

DISABLED INFORMATION

Wheelchairs: 160 spaces available in total
Helpers: Admitted
Prices: Free for the disabled. Helpers normal prices
Disabled Toilets: Available
Are Bookings Necessary: Yes
Contact: (0141) 632-1275

Travelling Supporters' Information:
Routes: From the South: Take the A724 to the Cambuslang Road and at Eastfield branch left into Main Street and follow through Burnhill Street and Westmuir Place into Prospecthill Road. Turn left into Aikenhead Road and right into Mount Annan for Kinghorn Drive and the Stadium; From the South: Take the A77 Fenwick Road, through Kilmarnock Road into Pollokshaws Road then turn right into Langside Avenue. Pass through Battle Place to Battlefield Road and turn left into Cathcart Road. Turn right into Letherby Drive, right into Carmunnock Road and 1st left into Mount Annan Drive for the Stadium; From the North & East: Exit M8 Junction 15 and passing Infirmary on left proceed into High Street and cross the Albert Bridge into Crown Street. Join Cathcart Road and proceed South until it becomes Carmunnock Road. Turn left into Mount Annan Drive and left again into Kinghorn Drive for the Stadium.

RAITH ROVERS FC

Founded: 1883 (**Entered League:** 1902)
Former Names: None
Nickname: 'The Rovers'
Ground: Stark's Park, Pratt Street,
Kirkcaldy KY1 1SA
Record Attendance: 31,306 (7/2/53)
Pitch Size: 113 × 67 yards

Colours: Shirts – Navy with White Trim
   Shorts – White with Navy Trim
Telephone Nº: (01592) 263514
Ticket Office: (01592) 263514
Fax Number: (01592) 642833
Ground Capacity: 10,105 (all seats)

SOUTH STAND

MAIN STAND | RAILWAY STAND (Away)

(Away)
NORTH STAND
KINCARDINE BRIDGE ROAD

GENERAL INFORMATION
Supporters Club: F. Hamilton, 22 Tower Terrace, Kirkcaldy
Telephone Nº: (01592) 653927
Car Parking: Esplanade and Beveridge Car Park
Coach Parking: Railway Station & Esplanade
Nearest Railway Station: Kirkcaldy (15 mins. walk)
Nearest Bus Station: Kirkcaldy (15 minutes walk)
Club Shop: At the ground (matchdays only) and also at Sports Division, Retail Park, Kirkcaldy
Opening Times: Open 7 days a week
Telephone Nº: (01592) 263514
Postal Sales: Yes
Nearest Police Station: St. Brycedale Road, Kirkcaldy (15 minutes walk)
Police Telephone Nº: (01592) 418700

GROUND INFORMATION
Away Supporters' Entrances & Sections:
North Stand and part of the Railway Stand

ADMISSION INFO (2000/2001 PRICES)
Adult Seating: £12.00
Child Seating: £5.00
Programme Price: £1.50

DISABLED INFORMATION
Wheelchairs: 12 spaces each for home and away fans accommodated in the North & South Stands
Helpers: One helper admitted per wheelchair
Prices: Free of charge for the disabled. Helpers pay the concessionary price
Disabled Toilets: Available in North & South Stands
Are Bookings Necessary: Only for all-ticket games
Contact: (01592) 263514

Web site: www.raithrovers.com

Travelling Supporters' Information:
Routes: Take the M8 to the end then follow the A90/M90 over the Forth Road Bridge. Exit the M90 at Junction 1 and follow the A921 to Kirkcaldy. On the outskirts of tow, turn left at the B & Q roundabout from which the floodlights can be seen. The ground is raised on the hill nearby.

RANGERS FC

Founded: 1873 (**Entered League:** 1890)	**Colours:** Shirts – Blue with White Trim
Former Names: None	Shorts – White
Nickname: 'The Gers' or 'Light Blues'	**Telephone Nº:** (0870) 600-1972
Ground: Ibrox Stadium, 150 Edmiston	**Ticket Office:** (0870) 600-1993
Drive, Glasgow G51 2XD	**Fax Number:** (0870) 600-1978
Record Attendance: 118,567 (2/1/39)	**Ground Capacity:** 50,467 (All seats)
Pitch Size: 125 × 89 yards	

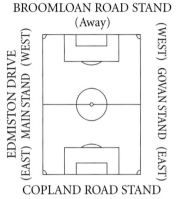

BROOMLOAN ROAD STAND
(Away)

EDMISTON DRIVE (EAST)   MAIN STAND (WEST)

(WEST) GOVAN STAND (EAST)

COPLAND ROAD STAND

GENERAL INFORMATION

Supporters Club: The Secretary, Rangers Supporters' Association, 250 Edmiston Drive, Glasgow
Telephone Nº: (0141) 427-4593
Car Parking: Albion Car Park
Coach Parking: By Police direction
Nearest Railway Station: Ibrox (Underground) – 2 minutes walk
Nearest Bus Station: Glasgow City Centre
Club Shop: The Rangers Superstore, Ibrox Stadium
Opening Times: Monday to Saturday 9.00am to 5.30pm; Sundays 11.00am to 5.00pm and also open one hour after the end of the game
Telephone Nº: (0141) 427-3710
Postal Sales: Yes – Rangers Direct (0990) 991997
Nearest Police Station: Strathclyde Police G Div., 923 Helen Street
Police Telephone Nº: (0141) 445-1113

GROUND INFORMATION

Away Supporters' Entrances & Sections:
Broomloan Road Turnstiles for Broomloan Road Stand

ADMISSION INFO (2000/2001 PRICES)

Adult Seating: £17.00 – £22.00
Child Seating: £10.00 – £11.00
Other Concessions: £13.00 – £15.00
Note: Most of the ground capacity is taken by season-ticket holders
Programme Price: £2.00

DISABLED INFORMATION

Wheelchairs: 60 spaces for home fans, 5 for away fans in front of the West Enclosure
Helpers: Admitted
Prices: Free of charge for the disabled and helpers if they are members of the Disabled Supporters' Club
Disabled Toilets: Available in the West Enclosure
Are Bookings Necessary: Yes
Contact: (0141) 427-8500

Web site: www.rangers.co.uk

Travelling Supporters' Information:
Routes: From All Parts: Exit the M8 at Junction 23. The road leads straight to the Stadium.

ROSS COUNTY FC

Founded: 1929 (**Entered League:** 1994)	**Colours:** Shirts – Navy Blue
Former Names: None	Shorts – White
Nickname: 'The County'	**Telephone N°:** (01349) 860860
Ground: Victoria Park, Dingwall,	**Ticket Office:** (01349) 860860
Ross-shire IV15 9QW	**Fax Number:** (01349) 866277
Record Attendance: 10,000 (19/2/66)	**Ground Capacity:** 6,500
Pitch Size: 110 × 72 yards	**Seating Capacity:** 1,519

GENERAL INFORMATION

Supporters Club: B. Campbell, c/o Victoria Park
Telephone N°: (01349) 862253
Car Parking: At the ground
Coach Parking: At the ground
Nearest Railway Station: Dingwall (adjacent)
Nearest Bus Station: Dingwall
Club Shop: At ground
Opening Times: Weekdays and Matchdays
Telephone N°: (01349) 862253
Postal Sales: Yes
Nearest Police Station: Dingwall
Police Telephone N°: (01349) 862444

GROUND INFORMATION

Away Supporters' Entrances & Sections:
East Stand entrances and accommodation

ADMISSION INFO (2000/2001 PRICES)

Adult Standing: £9.00
Adult Seating: £11.00
Child Standing: £4.00
Child Seating: £5.00
Programme Price: £1.00

DISABLED INFORMATION

Wheelchairs: 6 spaces each for home and away fans
Helpers: Admitted
Prices: Normal prices are charged
Disabled Toilets: Available at the bottom of the West Stand
Are Bookings Necessary: Yes
Contact: (01349) 862253

Travelling Supporters' Information:
Routes: The ground is situated at Dingwall adjacent to the Railway Station which is down Jubilee Park Road at the bottom of the High Street.

St. Johnstone FC

Founded: 1884 (**Entered League**: 1911)	**Colours**: Shirts – Blue
Former Names: None	Shorts – White
Nickname: 'Saints'	**Telephone Nº**: (01738) 459090
Ground: McDiarmid Park, Crieff Road,	**Ticket Office**: (01738) 459090
Perth PH1 2SJ	**Fax Number**: (01738) 625771
Record Attendance: 10,545 (23/5/99)	**Ground Capacity**: 10,721 (All seats)
Pitch Size: 115 × 75 yards	

ORMOND STAND
(FAMILY STAND)

EAST STAND

WEST STAND
(MAIN STAND)

(Away)
NORTH STAND

GENERAL INFORMATION

Supporters Club: J. McLeish, 157 Dunkeld Road, Perth PH1 3AE
Telephone Nº: (01738) 442022
Car Parking: Car park at the ground
Coach Parking: At the ground
Nearest Railway Station: Perth (3 miles)
Nearest Bus Station: Perth (3 miles)
Club Shop: At ground
Opening Times: 9.00am to 5.00pm
Telephone Nº: (01738) 459090
Postal Sales: Yes
Nearest Police Station: Perth (1½ miles)
Police Telephone Nº: (01738) 621141

GROUND INFORMATION

Away Supporters' Entrances & Sections:
North Stand Side entrances for accommodation in the North Stand and North End of the West Stand

ADMISSION INFO (2000/2001 PRICES)

Adult Seating: £12.00 – £16.00
Child Seating: £6.00 – £10.00
Note: Reduced rates available in the Family Stand
Programme Price: £1.50

DISABLED INFORMATION

Wheelchairs: 10 spaces each available for home and away fans in the East and West Stands
Helpers: Please phone the club for details
Prices: Please phone the club for details
Disabled Toilets: 2 available in both the East and West Stands
Are Bookings Necessary: Yes
Contact: (01738) 459090

Web site: www.stjohnstonefc.co.uk

Travelling Supporters' Information:
Routes: Follow the M80 to Stirling, take the A9 Inverness Road north from Perth and follow the signs for the 'Football Stadium'. The ground is situated beside a dual-carriageway – the Perth Western By-pass near Junction 11 of the M90.

ST. MIRREN FC

Founded: 1877 (**Entered League:** 1890)
Former Names: None
Nickname: 'The Saints' or 'The Buddies'
Ground: St. Mirren Park, Love Street, Paisley PA3 2EJ
Record Attendance: 47,428 (7/3/25)
Pitch Size: 110 × 70 yards

Colours: Shirts – Black and White Stripes Shorts – White
Telephone Nº: (0141) 889-2558
Ticket Office: (0141) 889-2558
Fax Number: (0141) 848-6444
Ground Capacity: 15,410
Seating Capacity: 9,395

WEST STAND (Away)

(ALBION STREET) MAIN STAND

NORTH STAND

WEST EAST

EAST STAND

GENERAL INFORMATION

Supporters Club: Ian Cuthbertson, Knox Street, Paisley
Telephone Nº: (0141) 887-2101
Car Parking: Street Parking
Coach Parking: Clark Street (off Greenock Road – 300 yards)
Nearest Railway Station: Paisley Gilmour Street (400 yards)
Nearest Bus Station: Paisley
Club Shop: In the West Stand
Opening Times: Daily from 8.00am to 10.00pm ??
Telephone Nº: (0141) 840-1337
Postal Sales: Yes
Nearest Police Station: Mill Street, Paisley (1 mile)
Police Telephone Nº: (0141) 889-1113

GROUND INFORMATION

Away Supporters' Entrances & Sections:
Entrances on West of Main Stand for West Stand

ADMISSION INFO (2000/2001 PRICES)

Adult Standing: £9.00
Adult Seating: £10.00 – £11.00
Child Standing: £4.50
Child Seating: £5.00 – £5.50
Note: Additional child concessions are available for early arrival
Programme Price: £1.50

DISABLED INFORMATION

Wheelchairs: Accommodated in the West Stand
Helpers: Admitted
Prices: Free of charge for both disabled and helpers
Disabled Toilets: 2 available in the West Stand
Are Bookings Necessary: Yes
Contact: (0141) 840-1337

Web site: www.stmirren.com

Travelling Supporters' Information:
Routes: From All Parts: Exit the M8 at Junction 29 and take the A726 Greenock Road. The ground is approximately ½ mile along on the left – the floodlights make it clearly visible from some distance.

STENHOUSEMUIR FC

Founded: 1884 **(Entered League:** 1921)
Former Names: Heather Rangers FC
Nickname: 'Warriors'
Ground: Ochilview Park, Gladstone
Road, Stenhousemuir FK5 5QL
Record Attendance: 12,500 (11/3/50)
Pitch Size: 110 × 72 yards

Colours: Shirts – Maroon
Shorts – White
Telephone N°: (01324) 562992
Ticket Office: (01324) 562992
Fax Number: (01324) 562980
Ground Capacity: 2,654
Seating Capacity: 628

TRYST ROAD

GENERAL INFORMATION
Supporters Club: A. McNeill, c/o Club
Telephone N°: (01324) 562992
Car Parking: Large Car Park adjacent
Coach Parking: Behind the North Terracing
Nearest Railway Station: Larbert (1 mile)
Nearest Bus Station: Falkirk (2½ miles)
Club Shop: At ground
Opening Times: Weekdays from 9.00am to 5.00pm
and also 1 hour before and after home games
Telephone N°: (01324) 562992
Postal Sales: Yes
Nearest Police Station: Stenhousemuir (½ mile)
Police Telephone N°: (01324) 562112

GROUND INFORMATION
Away Supporters' Entrances & Sections:
Terracing entrances and accommodation

ADMISSION INFO (2000/2001 PRICES)
Adult Standing: £8.00
Adult Seating: £9.00
Senior Citizen/Child Standing: £4.00
Senior Citizen/Child Seating: £4.50
Note: Additional Family Discounts are available
Programme Price: £1.50

DISABLED INFORMATION
Wheelchairs: Accommodated
Helpers: Admitted
Prices: Normal prices are charged
Disabled Toilets: Available in the New Gladstone
Road Stand
Are Bookings Necessary: No
Contact: (01324) 562992

Travelling Supporters' Information:
Routes: Exit the M876 at Junction 2 and follow signs for Stenhousemuir. Pass the Old Hospital and turn right after the Golf Course. The ground is on the left behind the houses – the floodlights are visible for ¼ mile.

STIRLING ALBION FC

Founded: 1945 (**Entered League:** 1946)
Former Names: None
Nickname: 'The Albion'
Ground: Forth Bank Stadium, Spring Kerse, Stirling   FK7 7UJ
Record Attendance: 3,808 (17/2/96)
Pitch Size: 110 × 74 yards

Colours: Shirts – Red and White stripes
Shorts – Red
Telephone N°: (01786) 450399
Ticket Office: (01786) 450399
Fax Number: (01786) 448592
Ground Capacity: 3,808
Seating Capacity: 2,500

NORTH TERRACING

WEST STAND

EAST STAND

(Away)
SOUTH TERRACING

GENERAL INFORMATION
Supporters Club: S. Torrance, c/o Club
Telephone N°: –
Car Parking: Large Car Park adjacent to the ground
Coach Parking: Adjacent to the ground
Nearest Railway Station: Stirling (2 miles)
Nearest Bus Station: Stirling (2 miles)
Club Shop: Yes
Opening Times: Matchdays Only
Telephone N°: (01786) 450399
Postal Sales: Yes
Nearest Police Station: Stirling (2 miles)
Police Telephone N°: (01786) 456000

GROUND INFORMATION
Away Supporters' Entrances & Sections:
South Terracing entrances and accommodation.

ADMISSION INFO (2000/2001 PRICES)
Adult Standing: £8.00
Adult Seating: £9.00
Child Standing: £4.00
Child Seating: £5.00
Note: Standing admission is only available for certain games
Programme Price: £1.00

DISABLED INFORMATION
Wheelchairs: 18 spaces available each for home and away fans
Helpers: Admitted
Prices: Free of charge for the disabled
Disabled Toilets: 2 available beneath each stand
Are Bookings Necessary: No
Contact: (01786) 450399

Web site: www.stirlingalbionfc.co.uk

Travelling Supporters' Information:
Routes: Follow signs for Stirling from the M9/M80 Northbound. From Pirnhall Roundabout follow signs for Alloa/St. Andrew's to the 4th roundabout and then turn left for the stadium.

STRANRAER FC

Founded: 1870 (**Entered League:** 1955)	**Colours:** Shirts – Blue
Former Names: None	Shorts – White
Nickname: 'The Blues'	**Telephone Nº:** (01776) 703271
Ground: Stair Park, London Road,	**Ticket Office:** (01776) 703271
Stranraer DG9 8BS	**Fax Number:** (01776) 702194
Record Attendance: 6,500 (24/1/48)	**Ground Capacity:** 5,500
Pitch Size: 110 × 70 yards	**Seating Capacity:** 1,900

GENERAL INFORMATION

Supporters Club: Mrs. Margaret Rennie, 18 Eastwood Avenue, Stranraer
Telephone Nº: (01776) 706563
Car Parking: Car Park at the ground
Coach Parking: Port Rodie, Stranraer
Nearest Railway Station: Stranraer (1 mile)
Nearest Bus Station: Port Rodie, Stranraer
Club Shop: At the ground
Opening Times: 2.30pm to 3.00pm and during half-time on Matchdays only
Telephone Nº: –
Postal Sales: Write to 28 Springfield Crescent, Stranraer
Nearest Police Station: Stranraer (¾ mile)
Police Telephone Nº: (01776) 702112

GROUND INFORMATION

Away Supporters' Entrances & Sections:
London Road entrances for the Visitors Stand

ADMISSION INFO (2000/2001 PRICES)

Adult Standing: £8.00
Adult Seating: £10.00
Child Standing: £4.00
Child Seating: £6.00
Programme Price: £1.00

DISABLED INFORMATION

Wheelchairs: 6 spaces each for Home and Away fans in front of the North Stand and South Stand
Helpers: Please phone the club for details
Prices: Please phone the club for details
Disabled Toilets: One available each in the North and South Stands
Are Bookings Necessary: Yes
Contact: (01776) 702194

Web site: www.stranraerfc.co.uk

Travelling Supporters' Information:
Routes: From the West: Take the A75 to Stranraer and the ground is on the left-hand side of the road in a public park shortly after entering the town; From the North: Take the A77 and follow it to where it joins with the A75 (then as West). The ground is set back from the road and the floodlights are clearly visible.

THE HIGHLAND FOOTBALL LEAGUE

Founded
1893

Secretary
Mr. J.H. Grant

Address
35 Hamilton Drive, Elgin   IV30 2NN

Phone
(01343) 544995

BRORA RANGERS FC

Founded: 1878/79
Former Names: None
Nickname: 'The Cattachs'
Ground: Dudgeon Park, Brora, KW9 6QA
Record Attendance: 2,000 (31/8/63)
Colours: Shirts – Red with White Pin Stripes
Shorts – White

Telephone Nº: (01408) 621570
Fax Number: (01408) 621231
Ground Capacity: 4,000
Seating Capacity: 250
Pitch Size: 112 × 70 yards
Contact Phone Nº: (01408) 621231

SCHOOL END

MAIN STAND

SEAFORTH ENCLOSURE

SOCIAL CLUB
CAR PARK

GENERAL INFORMATION
Supporters Club: c/o Club
Telephone Nº: (01408) 621570
Car Parking: Adjacent to the ground
Coach Parking: Adjacent to the ground
Nearest Railway Station: Brora
Nearest Bus Station: Brora
Club Shop: At the ground
Opening Times: Matchdays Only
Telephone Nº: (01408) 621231
Postal Sales: Yes
Nearest Police Station: Brora
Police Telephone Nº: (01408) 621222

GROUND INFORMATION
Away Supporters' Entrances & Sections:
No usual segregation

ADMISSION INFO (2000/2001 PRICES)
Adult Standing: £4.00
Adult Seating: £4.50
Child Standing: £2.00
Child Seating: £2.50
Programme Price: 50p

DISABLED INFORMATION
Wheelchairs: Accommodated
Helpers: Please phone the club for details
Prices: Please phone the club for details
Disabled Toilets: None
Are Bookings Necessary: Yes
Contact: (01408) 621231

Travelling Supporters' Information:
Routes: Take the A9 Northbound from Inverness and the Stadium is situated on the right upon entering the town. It is clearly visible from the road.

BUCKIE THISTLE FC

Founded: 1889	**Telephone Nº:** (01542) 836468
Former Names: None	**Fax Number:** None
Nickname: 'The Jags'	**Pitch Size:** 109 × 73 yards
Ground: Victoria Park, Mid Mar Street, Buckie, Banffshire	**Ground Capacity:** 5,400
Record Attendance: 8,600 (1/3/58)	**Seating Capacity:** 400
Colours: Shirts – Green and White Hoops Shorts – White	**Contact Address:** Easton Thain (Sec.), Flat 5, Milton Lodge, Seafield Avenue, Keith AB55 5BS
	Contact Nº: (01542) 886141 (Evenings)

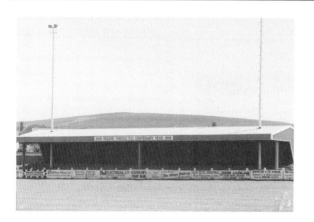

SCHOOL END

GENERAL INFORMATION
Supporters Club: Yes – c/o Club
Telephone Nº: –
Car Parking: Adjacent to the ground
Coach Parking: Adjacent to the ground
Nearest Railway Station: Keith (12 miles)
Nearest Bus Station: Buckie
Club Shop: None
Social Club: Buckie Thistle Social Club, 3/5 West Church Street, Buckie
Social Club Telephone Nº: (01542) 832894
Nearest Police Station: Buckie
Police Telephone Nº: (01542) 832222

GROUND INFORMATION
Away Supporters' Entrances & Sections:
No usual segregation

ADMISSION INFO (1999/2000 PRICES)
Adult Standing: £4.00
Adult Seating: £4.00
Concessions Standing: £2.00
Concessions Seating: £2.00
Programme Price: 50p

DISABLED INFORMATION
Wheelchairs: Accommodated when required, but no specific facilities
Helpers: Admitted
Prices: Normal prices apply
Disabled Toilets: None – but available within 100 yards of the ground
Are Bookings Necessary: No – but useful
Contact: (01542) 886141

Travelling Supporters' Information:
Routes: Take the A98 towards Cullen and turn left at Drybridge Crossroads for Buckie Town Centre. After ½ mile, turn left into West Cathcart Street, then left via South Pringle Street to Victoria Park. The ground is situated at the junction of South Pringle Street and Mid Mar Street.

CLACHNACUDDIN FC

Founded: 1886
Former Names: None
Nickname: 'Lilywhites'
Ground: Grant Street Park, Wyvis Place, Inverness IV3 6DR
Record Attendance: 9,000 (27/8/51)
Colours: Shirts – White
Shorts – Black

Telephone Nº: (01463) 238825
Ticket Information: (01463) 710707
Fax Number: (01463) 718261
Ground Capacity: 3,000
Seating Capacity: 154
Pitch Size: 108 × 70 yards
Contact Address: P. Corbett, c/o Club
Contact Phone Nº: (01463) 710707

SOCIAL CLUB

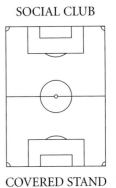

COVERED STAND

GENERAL INFORMATION
Supporters Club: None
Telephone Nº: –
Car Parking: Adjacent to the ground
Coach Parking: Adjacent to the ground
Nearest Railway Station: Inverness
Nearest Bus Station: Inverness
Club Shop: At the ground
Opening Times: Matchdays Only
Telephone Nº: (01463) 710707
Postal Sales: Yes
Nearest Police Station: Inverness
Police Telephone Nº: (01463) 239191

GROUND INFORMATION
Away Supporters' Entrances & Sections:
No usual segregation

ADMISSION INFO (2000/2001 PRICES)
Adult Standing: £4.00
Adult Seating: £5.00
Child Standing: £2.00
Child Seating: £2.50
Programme Price: 20p

DISABLED INFORMATION
Wheelchairs: Accommodated
Helpers: Admitted
Prices: Normal prices apply
Disabled Toilets: Yes
Are Bookings Necessary: No
Contact: No

Travelling Supporters' Information:
Routes: From the East and South: From the roundabout at the junction of the A9 and A96, proceed into the Town Centre and over the River Ness. Turning right at the traffic lights (onto A862 to Dingwall) up Kenneth Street, over the roundabout onto Telford Street for 200 yards turning right into Telford Road opposite Fish Shop. At the top, turn left on Lower Kessack Street and left again. Left into Wyvis Place, ground is on the left.

COVE RANGERS FC

Founded: 1922
Former Names: None
Nickname: None
Ground: Allan Park, Loirston Road, Cove, Aberdeen   AB12 4NS
Record Attendance: 2,300 (15/11/92)
Colours: Shirts – Blue
              Shorts – Blue

Telephone Nº: (01224) 871467 (Social Club)
Fax Number: (01224) 879023/895199
Ground Capacity: 2,300
Seating Capacity: 200
Pitch Size: 104× 65 yards
Contact Address: Duncan Little, c/o Club
Contact Phone Nº: (01224) 890433 (Club)
Social Club Nº: (01224) 871467

COVERED ENCLOSURE

MAIN STAND

OPEN TERRACING

GENERAL INFORMATION

Supporters Club: Brian Dean, c/o Social Club, Allan Park, Cove, Aberdeen
Telephone Nº: (01224) 871467
Car Parking: School Car Park/Loirston Road
Coach Parking: By Police Direction
Nearest Railway Station: Guild Street, Aberdeen
Nearest Bus Station: Guild Street, Aberdeen
Club Shop: At the Social Club
Opening Times: Matchdays Only
Telephone Nº: (01224) 871467
Postal Sales: Via Ian Armstrong, c/o Club
Nearest Police Station: Nigg Sub Station
Police Telephone Nº: (01224) 639111

GROUND INFORMATION

Away Supporters' Entrances & Sections:
Loirston Road entrances and accommodation

ADMISSION INFO (2000/2001 PRICES)

Adult Standing: £4.00
Adult Seating: £4.00
Child Standing: £2.00
Child Seating: £2.00
Programme Price: 50p

DISABLED INFORMATION

Wheelchairs: Accommodated
Helpers: Admitted
Prices: Normal prices apply
Disabled Toilets: Available in the Social Club
Are Bookings Necessary: No, but preferable
Contact: (01224) 890433 (Duncan Little) (Matchdays); (01224) 896282 (Evenings)

Travelling Supporters' Information:
Routes: From the North: Follow signs to Altens and Cove and take the Cove turn-off at the Skean Dhu Hotel roundabout along Loirston Road – Ground is ½ mile on the right; From the South: Take the Aberdeen Harbour turn-off some 10 miles north of Stonehaven and continue to Skean Dhu Hotel roundabout – then as North.
Bus Routes: No. 13 bus runs from City Centre to Ground.

DEVERONVALE FC

Founded: 1938	**Telephone Nº:** (01261) 818489
Former Names: None	**Fax Number:** (01261) 818489
Nickname: 'The Vale'	**Ground Capacity:** 2,600
Ground: Princess Royal Park, Airlie	**Seating Capacity:** 300
Gardens, Banff AB45 1HD	**Pitch Size:** 109 × 78 yards
Record Attendance: 5,000 (27/4/52)	**Contact Address:** Stewart McPherson,
Colours: Shirts – Red with White trim	19 Reid Street, Banff AB45 1HJ
Shorts – White	**Contact Phone Nº:** (01261) 818489

BRIDGE STREET END

MAIN STAND

CANAL PARK BANK

NEW ROAD END

GENERAL INFORMATION

Supporters Club: The Secretary, c/o The Railway Inn, North Castle Street, Banff
Telephone Nº: (01261) 812251
Car Parking: Street Parking
Coach Parking: Bridge Road Car Park
Nearest Railway Station: Keith (20 miles)
Nearest Bus Station: Macduff (1 mile)
Club Shop: At the ground
Opening Times: Matchdays Only
Telephone Nº: (01261) 818489
Postal Sales: Yes
Nearest Police Station: Banff
Police Telephone Nº: (01261) 812555

GROUND INFORMATION

Away Supporters' Entrances & Sections:
No usual segregation

ADMISSION INFO (2000/2001 PRICES)

Adult Standing: £4.00
Adult Seating: £5.00
Child Standing: £2.00
Child Seating: £3.00
Programme Price: 50p

DISABLED INFORMATION

Wheelchairs: Accommodated
Helpers: Admitted
Prices: Please phone the club for details
Disabled Toilets: None
Are Bookings Necessary: Yes
Contact: (01261) 818489

Web site: www.deveronvale.freeserve.co.uk

Travelling Supporters' Information:
Routes: From Aberdeen: Take the first exit on the right after Banff Bridge – the ground is ½ mile on the left. From Inverness: Travel through Banff on the main by-pass and take the left turn before Banff Bridge – the ground is ½ mile on the left.

FORRES MECHANICS FC

Founded: 1884
Former Names: None
Nickname: 'Can Cans'
Ground: Mosset Park, Lea Road, Forres IV36 0AU
Record Attendance: 7,000 (2/2/57)
Colours: Shirts – Maroon & Gold stripes Shorts – Maroon

Telephone/Fax Number: (01309) 675096
Ground Capacity: 6,540
Seating Capacity: 540
Pitch Size: 106 × 69 yards
Contact Address: C.C. Fraser, 19 Pilmuir Road West, Forres IV36 0HN
Contact Phone Nº: (01309) 672349

BOGTON END

CAR PARK STAND

GAS WORKS END

GENERAL INFORMATION

Supporters Club: Paul Wilson, 141c High Street, Forres
Telephone Nº: (01309) 675784
Car Parking: At the ground
Coach Parking: At the ground
Nearest Railway Station: Forres
Nearest Bus Station: Forres
Club Shop: At the ground
Opening Times: Matchdays only
Telephone Nº: (01309) 675096
Postal Sales: –
Nearest Police Station: Forres
Police Telephone Nº: (01309) 672224

GROUND INFORMATION

Away Supporters' Entrances & Sections:
No usual segregation

ADMISSION INFO (2000/2001 PRICES)

Adult Standing: £4.00
Adult Seating: £5.00
Child/O.A.P. Standing: £2.00
Child/O.A.P. Seating: £3.00
Programme Price: 80p

DISABLED INFORMATION

Wheelchairs: Accommodated
Helpers: Admitted
Prices: Normal prices apply
Disabled Toilets: One available
Are Bookings Necessary: No
Contact: (01309) 675096

Travelling Supporters' Information:
Routes: Exit the Forres Bypass (A940) for Grantown on Spey/Forres Town Centre. Take the first left along the burn, cross the bridge then first left for the ground. The Stand is clearly visible from the Bypass.

FORT WILLIAM FC

Founded: 1984
Former Names: None
Nickname: 'The Fort'
Ground: Claggan Park, Fort William, Inverness-shire
Record Attendance: 1,500 (4/1/86)
Colours: Shirts – Gold and Black
Shorts – Black
Telephone Nº: None at the ground

Ground Capacity: 4,600
Seating Capacity: 400
Pitch Size: 102 × 80 yards
Contact Address: J. Baird, 11 Clerk Drive, Corpach, Fort William   PH33 6LZ
Contact Phone Nº: (01397) 708000
Contact Fax Number: (01397) 705627
Social Club Number: (01397) 703829

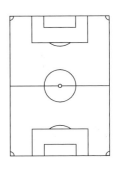

GENERAL INFORMATION
Supporters Club: None
Telephone Nº: –
Car Parking: At the ground
Coach Parking: At the ground
Nearest Railway Station: Fort William
Nearest Bus Station: Fort William
Club Shop: None
Opening Times: –
Telephone Nº: –
Postal Sales: –
Nearest Police Station: High Street, Fort William
Police Telephone Nº: (01397) 702361

GROUND INFORMATION
Away Supporters' Entrances & Sections:
No usual segregation

ADMISSION INFO (2000/2001 PRICES)
Adult Standing: £4.00
Adult Seating: £4.00
Child Standing: £2.00
Child Seating: £2.00
Programme Price: None

DISABLED INFORMATION
Wheelchairs: Accommodated
Helpers: Please phone the club for details
Prices: Please phone the club for details
Disabled Toilets: None
Are Bookings Necessary: No
Contact: (01397) 708000

Travelling Supporters' Information:
Routes: From the South: Approaching Fort William on the A82, proceed on the Bypass of the Town Centre. After 2 roundabouts continue on Belford Road past the Railway Station on the left and the Swimming Baths on the right. After ½ mile and crossing over the River Nevis, take the first right into Claggan Road and the ground is ½ mile on the left.

FRASERBURGH FC

Founded: 1910	**Telephone Nº:** (01346) 518444
Former Names: None	**Fax Number:** (01346) 511822
Nickname: 'The Broch'	**Ground Capacity:** 4,500
Ground: Bellslea Park, Seaforth Street,	**Seating Capacity:** 480
Fraserburgh AB43 9BD	**Pitch Size:** 106 × 66 yards
Record Attendance: 5,800 (13/2/54)	**Contact Address:** Finlay Noble,
Colours: Shirts – Black and White Stripes	18 Bawdley Head, Fraserburgh AB43 9SE
Shorts – Black	**Contact Phone Nº:** (01346) 518444

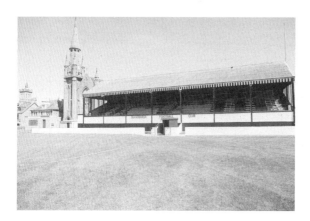
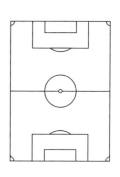

GENERAL INFORMATION

Supporters Club: David Henderson, 3 Lewis Place, Fraserburgh AB43 9WU
Telephone Nº: (01346) 516693
Car Parking: At the ground
Coach Parking: At the ground
Nearest Railway Station: Aberdeen (40 miles)
Nearest Bus Station: Fraserburgh
Club Shop: At the ground
Opening Times: Matchdays Only
Telephone Nº: (01346) 518444
Postal Sales: Yes
Web site: www.burghfc.demon.co.uk
Nearest Police Station: Fraserburgh
Police Telephone Nº: (01346) 513121

GROUND INFORMATION

Away Supporters' Entrances & Sections:
No usual segregation

ADMISSION INFO (2000/2001 PRICES)

Adult Standing: £4.00
Adult Seating: £4.50
Child Standing: £2.00
Child Seating: £2.50
Programme Price: £1.00

DISABLED INFORMATION

Wheelchairs: Accommodated
Helpers: Admitted
Prices: Normal prices apply
Disabled Toilets: Yes
Are Bookings Necessary: No
Contact: (01346) 518444

Web site: www.burghfc.demon.co.uk

Travelling Supporters' Information:
Routes: The ground is situated in the Town Centre, off Seaforth Street.

HUNTLY FC

Founded: 1928	**Telephone Nº:** (01466) 793548
Former Names: None	**Fax Number:** None
Nickname: None	**Ground Capacity:** 4,500
Ground: Christie Park, East Park Street,	**Seating Capacity:** 270
Huntly, Aberdeenshire AB54 8JE	**Pitch Size:** 105 × 72 yards
Record Attendance: 4,500 (18/2/95)	**Contact Address:** Peter Morrison, Glenlea,
Colours: Shirts – Black and Gold	Littlejohn Street, Huntly AB54 8HL
Shorts – Black	**Contact Phone Nº:** (01466) 793269

EAST PARK STREET

COVERED ENCLOSURE

STAND

GENERAL INFORMATION
Social Club: Within the ground
Telephone Nº: (01466) 793680
Car Parking: At the ground
Coach Parking: At the ground
Nearest Railway Station: Huntly (1 mile)
Nearest Bus Station: Huntly (¼ mile)
Club Shop: At the ground
Opening Times: Matchdays Only
Telephone Nº: –   **Postal Sales:** –
Web site: www.huntlyfc.co.uk
Nearest Police Station: Adjacent to the ground
Police Telephone Nº: (01466) 792246

GROUND INFORMATION
Away Supporters' Entrances & Sections:
No usual segregation

ADMISSION INFO (2000/2001 PRICES)
Adult Standing: £4.00
Adult Seating: £5.00
Child Standing: £2.50
Child Seating: £3.50
Programme Price: £1.00

DISABLED INFORMATION
Wheelchairs: Accommodated
Helpers: Please phone the club for details
Prices: Please phone the club for details
Disabled Toilets: None
Are Bookings Necessary: No
Contact: (01466) 793269

Travelling Supporters' Information:
Routes: Enter the Town off the A96 and proceed along King George V Avenue and Gordon Street. Pass through the Town Centre Square, along Castle Street to East Park Street and the ground is on the right before the Castle.

KEITH FC

Founded: 1919	**Telephone N°:** (01542) 887407 (matchdays)
Former Names: None	**Fax Number:** (01542) 882629
Nickname: 'Maroons'	**Ground Capacity:** 4,500
Ground: Kynoch Park, Balloch Road,	**Seating Capacity:** 450
Keith AB55 5EN	**Pitch Size:** 110 × 75 yards
Record Attendance: 5,820 (4/2/28)	**Correspondence Address:**
Colours: Shirts – Maroon with Sky Blue	Alex Rutherford, c/o Club
Shorts – Maroon with Sky Blue	**Contact Phone N°:** (01542) 882629

GENERAL INFORMATION

Supporters Club: None
Telephone N°: –
Car Parking: Street parking in Balloch Road, Moss Street and Reidhaven Square
Coach Parking: Balloch Road or Bridge Street Coach Park
Nearest Railway Station: Keith (1 mile)
Nearest Bus Station: Keith
Club Shop: At the ground
Opening Times: Wednesdays and Thursdays 9.00am to 4.00pm; Fridays 9.00am – 12.30pm
Telephone N°: (01542) 882629
Postal Sales: Yes
Nearest Police Station: Turner Street, Keith
Police Telephone N°: (01542) 882502

GROUND INFORMATION

Away Supporters' Entrances & Sections:
No usual segregation except for some Cup Ties

ADMISSION INFO (2000/2001 PRICES)

Adult Standing: £4.00
Adult Seating: £5.00
Child Standing: £2.00
Child Seating: £3.00
Programme Price: 50p

DISABLED INFORMATION

Wheelchairs: Accommodated
Helpers: Admitted
Prices: Normal prices apply
Disabled Toilets: None
Are Bookings Necessary: Yes
Contact: (01542) 886644

Travelling Supporters' Information:
Routes: From Aberdeen: Coming in on the A96, turn right up Bridge Street (across from the Bus Stop at Reidhaven Square), then take the first left for Balloch Road; From Inverness: Coming in on the A96, turn second left after the Citroen Keith Garage in Moss Street onto Balloch Road.

LOSSIEMOUTH FC

Founded: 1945	**Telephone Nº:** (01343) 813717
Former Names: None	**Fax Number:** (01343) 815440
Nickname: 'Coasters'	**Social Club Nº:** (01343) 813168
Ground: Grant Park, Kellas Avenue,	**Ground Capacity:** 3,500
Lossiemouth IV31 6JG	**Seating Capacity:** 250
Record Attendance: 2,700 (28/12/48)	**Contact Address:** Alan McIntosh,
Pitch Size: 110 × 60 yards	3 Forties Place, Lossiemouth IV31 6SS
Colours: Shirts – Red	**Contact Phone Nº:** (01343) 813328 and
Shorts – Red	(07967) 519384

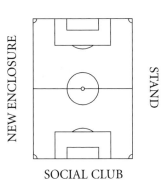

SOCIAL CLUB

GENERAL INFORMATION
Supporters Club: Neil Macpherson, 39-41 Malduff Street, Lossiemouth
Telephone Nº: (01343) 813168
Car Parking: At the ground
Coach Parking: At the ground
Nearest Railway Station: Elgin
Nearest Bus Station: Lossiemouth
Club Shop: At the ground
Opening Times: Matchdays Only
Telephone Nº: (01343) 813168
Postal Sales: Yes
Nearest Police Station: Lossiemouth
Police Telephone Nº: (01343) 812022

GROUND INFORMATION
Away Supporters' Entrances & Sections:
No usual segregation

ADMISSION INFO (2000/2001 PRICES)
Adult Standing: £4.00
Adult Seating: £4.00
Child Standing: £2.00
Child Seating: £2.00
Programme Price: 50p

DISABLED INFORMATION
Wheelchairs: Accommodated
Helpers: Admitted
Prices: Free of charge for the disabled
Disabled Toilets: Yes
Are Bookings Necessary: Yes
Contact: (01343) 813328 (Alan McIntosh)

Travelling Supporters' Information:
Routes: Take the Main Road into Lossiemouth and take the second turning on the right. Turn right again after 100 yards.

NAIRN COUNTY FC

Founded: 1914
Former Names: None
Nickname: 'The Wee County'
Ground: Station Park, Balblair Road, Nairn   IV12 5LT
Record Attendance: 4,000 (2/9/50)
Colours: Shirts – Yellow and Black
Shorts – Yellow

Telephone Nº: (01667) 454298
Fax Number: (01667) 462510
Ground Capacity: 3,800
Seating Capacity: 250
Pitch Size: 110 × 62 yards
Contact Address: John McNeill, 50 Station Road, Ardersier, Inverness   IV2 7ST
Contact Phone Nº: (01667) 462510

GENERAL INFORMATION
Supporters Club: Nairn County Social Club
Telephone Nº: (01667) 451504
Car Parking: At the ground
Coach Parking: At the ground
Nearest Railway Station: Nairn (adjacent)
Nearest Bus Station: King Street, Nairn (½ mile)
Club Shop: At the Social Club
Opening Times: Club Hours only
Telephone Nº: (01667) 453286
Postal Sales: Alex MacKintosh, c/o Social Club
Nearest Police Station: King Street, Nairn
Police Telephone Nº: (01667) 452222

GROUND INFORMATION
Away Supporters' Entrances & Sections:
No usual segregation

ADMISSION INFO (2000/2001 PRICES)
Adult Standing: £4.00
Adult Seating: £5.00
Child Standing: £2.00
Child Seating: £2.50
Programme Price: £1.00

DISABLED INFORMATION
Wheelchairs: Accommodated in the Stand
Helpers: Admitted
Prices: £4.00 for the disabled
Disabled Toilets: None
Are Bookings Necessary: No
Contact: (01667) 462510 (John McNeill)

Travelling Supporters' Information:
Routes: The ground is situated on the south side of Nairn at the bottom of the Main Street, adjacent to the Railway Station.

ROTHES FC

Founded: 1938
Former Names: Rothes Victoria FC
Nickname: 'The Speysiders'
Ground: Mackessack Park, Rothes, AB38
Record Attendance: 2,054 (September 1946)
Pitch Size: 108 × 74 yards
Colours: Shirts – Tangerine
　　　　　Shorts – Black

Telephone Nº: (01340) 831972
Social Club Nº: (01340) 831348
Fax Number: None
Ground Capacity: 2,650
Seating Capacity: 160
Contact Address: Neil R. McKenzie, c/o
Rothes FC Social Club, Seafield Square, Rothes
Contact Phone Nº: (01340) 831344

GENERAL INFORMATION
Supporters Club: None
Telephone Nº: –
Car Parking: At the ground
Coach Parking: At the ground
Nearest Railway Station: Elgin
Nearest Bus Station: Elgin
Club Shop: None
Opening Times: –
Telephone Nº: –
Postal Sales: –
Nearest Police Station: Rothes
Police Telephone Nº: (01340) 831341

GROUND INFORMATION
Away Supporters' Entrances & Sections:
No usual segregation

ADMISSION INFO (2000/2001 PRICES)
Adult Standing: £4.00
Adult Seating: £5.00
Child Standing: £2.00
Child Seating: £2.50
Programme Price: None – Monthly Magazine 50p

DISABLED INFORMATION
Wheelchairs: Accommodated
Helpers: Admitted
Prices: Normal prices apply
Disabled Toilets: None
Are Bookings Necessary: No
Contact: (01340) 831344 (Secretary)

Travelling Supporters' Information:
Routes: The ground is situated by Grant's Whisky Distillery at the North side of Rothes, by the junction of the Keith and Elgin Roads.

WICK ACADEMY FC

Founded: 1893	**Telephone Nº:** (01955) 602446
Former Names: None	**Fax Number:** (01955) 602446
Nickname: 'The Scorries'	**Ground Capacity:** 2,000
Ground: Harmsworth Park, South Road,	**Seating Capacity:** 433
Wick, Caithness KW1 5NH	**Pitch Size:** 106 × 76 yards
Record Attendance: 2,000 (30/7/84)	**Contact Address:** Mr. A. Carter, 8 Argyle
Colours: Shirts – Black and White Stripes	Square, Wick, Caithness KW1 5AL
Shorts – Black	**Contact Phone Nº:** (01955) 604275

GENERAL INFORMATION
Supporters Club: None
Telephone Nº: –
Car Parking: At the ground
Coach Parking: At the ground
Nearest Railway Station: Wick (10 minutes walk)
Nearest Bus Station: Wick
Club Shop: Wick Sports Shop, High Street, Wick
Opening Times: 9.00am to 5.00pm
Telephone Nº: (01955) 602930
Postal Sales: Yes
Nearest Police Station: Bridge Street, Wick
Police Telephone Nº: (01955) 603551

GROUND INFORMATION
Away Supporters' Entrances & Sections:
No usual segregation

ADMISSION INFO (2000/2001 PRICES)
Adult Standing: £4.00
Adult Seating: £5.00 (North Stand)
Child Standing: £2.00
Child Seating: £3.00 (North Stand)
Programme Price: 50p

DISABLED INFORMATION
Wheelchairs: 2 spaces available in the North Stand
Helpers: Please phone the club for details
Prices: Please phone the club for details
Disabled Toilets: None
Are Bookings Necessary: No
Contact: (01955) 604275

Travelling Supporters' Information:
Routes: The ground is situated on the A99 road from Inverness beside the Cemetery.

THE EAST OF SCOTLAND LEAGUE

Founded
1930

Secretary
Mr. J.M. Greenhorn

Address
2 Baberton Mains Court,
Edinburgh   EH14   3ER

Phone
(0131) 442-1402

ANNAN ATHLETIC FC

Founded: 1942
Former Names: Solway Star FC
Nickname: None
Ground: Galabank, North Street, Annan, Dumfries & Galloway
Record Attendance: 1,500
Colours: Shirts – Black & Gold Stripes
Shorts – Black

Telephone N°: (01461) 204108
Fax Number: (01461) 204108
Ground Capacity: 2,000
Seating Capacity: None
Pitch Size: 110 × 65 yards
Contact Address: A. Irving, Secretary, 1 Newlands Rise, Annan   DG12 5HT
Contact Phone N°: (01461) 203702 (home);   (01461) 207218 (business)

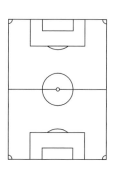

STAND

GENERAL INFORMATION
Supporters Club: None
Telephone N°: –
Car Parking: Available at the ground
Coach Parking: Available at the ground
Nearest Railway Station: Annan
Nearest Bus Station: Annan
Club Shop: Yes
Opening Times: Saturdays between 3.00pm and 6.00pm
Telephone N°: (01461) 204108
Postal Sales: Yes
Nearest Police Station: Annan
Police Telephone N°: –

GROUND INFORMATION
Away Supporters' Entrances & Sections:
No usual segregation

ADMISSION INFO (2000/2001 PRICES)
Adult Standing: £2.00
Child Standing: 50p
Programme Price: £1.00

DISABLED INFORMATION
Wheelchairs: Accommodated
Helpers: Please phone the club for details
Prices: Please phone the club for details
Disabled Toilets: Yes
Are Bookings Necessary: No
Contact: –

Travelling Supporters' Information:
Routes: From the East: Take the A75 to Annan. Approaching Annan, exit onto the B6357 (Stapleton Road) and after ¾ mile take the second exit at the roundabout into Scotts Street. Continue into Church Street and High Street. Turn right into Lady Street (B722) and following along into North Street for the Ground; From the West: Take the A75 to Annan and turn right onto B721 through Howes and into High Street in Annan (1 mile). After about 300 yards turn left into Lady Street. Then as above.

CIVIL SERVICE STROLLERS FC

Founded: 1908
Former Names: None
Nickname: 'Strollers'
Ground: Muirhouse Sports Ground,
Marine Drive, Edinburgh
Record Attendance: Unknown
Colours: Shirts – White with Dark Blue stripe
Shorts – Blue

Telephone Nº: (0131) 332-0650
Fax Number: None
Ground Capacity: 500 approximately
Seating Capacity: None
Pitch Size: 100 × 60 yards
Contact Address: W. Christie,
50 Craigleith Hill Avenue, Edinburgh
Contact Phone Nº: (0131) 332-3567

GENERAL INFORMATION

Supporters Club: None
Telephone Nº: –
Car Parking: At the ground
Coach Parking: At the ground
Nearest Railway Station: Edinburgh Waverley
Nearest Bus Station: St. Andrew's Square
Club Shop: None
Opening Times: –
Telephone Nº: –
Postal Sales: –
Nearest Police Station: Ferry Road, Edinburgh
Police Telephone Nº: (0131) 200-7211

ADMISSION INFO (1999/2000 PRICES)

No charge normally. For Scottish Cup games a charge of £2.00 for Adults and £1.00 for Children is made

DISABLED INFORMATION

Wheelchairs: Accommodated
Helpers: –
Prices: –
Disabled Toilets: None
Are Bookings Necessary: No
Contact: –

Travelling Supporters' Information:
Routes: From the West: Take the A90 Queensferry Road into Edinburgh and continue until reaching the B9085 (Quality Street). Turn left into Quality Street and continue into Cramond Road. After ¼ mile turn right into Lauriston Farm Road. Continue to the roundabout and go left along Silver Knowes Road then into Marine Drive for the Ground; From the East: Take the A1 into Edinburgh and at the 1st roundabout take the 2nd exit into Milton Link. At the next roundabout (¼ mile) take 2nd exit onto A199 Sir Harry Lauder Road. Continue along A199 for approximately 2½ miles past Leith then join the A901 (Lindsay Road). Continue along A901 to the end of Lower Granton Road then take the 3rd exit at the roundabout into West Granton Road and after 1¼ mile take the 3rd exit at the roundabout into Marine Drive.

COLDSTREAM FC

Founded: 1895	**Telephone Nº:** (01890) 883085
Former Names: None	**Fax Number:** (01890) 883085
Nickname: 'The Streamers'	**Ground Capacity:** 1,500
Ground: Home Park, Coldstream,	**Seating Capacity:** None
Berwickshire	**Pitch Size:** 100 × 60 yards
Record Attendance: Unknown	**Contact Address:** Rose Purvis,
Colours: Shirts – Royal Blue + black trim	35 Parkside, Coldstream, TD12 4DY
Shorts – Black	**Contact Phone Nº:** (01890) 882912

PAVILION END

HIGH STREET
END

GENERAL INFORMATION
Supporters Club: None
Telephone Nº: –
Car Parking: Adjacent to the ground
Coach Parking: Adajcent to the ground
Nearest Railway Station: Berwick-upon-Tweed
Nearest Bus Station: Kelso
Club Shop: At the ground
Opening Times: Match days only
Telephone Nº: –
Postal Sales: –
Nearest Police Station: Coldstream
Police Telephone Nº: (01890) 882402

GROUND INFORMATION
Away Supporters' Entrances & Sections:
No usual segregation

ADMISSION INFO (1999/2000 PRICES)
No charge normally. For Scottish Cup games a charge of £2.00 for Adults and £1.00 for Children is made

DISABLED INFORMATION
Wheelchairs: Accommodated
Helpers: –
Prices: –
Disabled Toilets: Available
Are Bookings Necessary: No
Contact: –

Travelling Supporters' Information:
Routes: From Edinburgh and the West: Take the A698 to Coldstream along Kelso Road into the High Street. After approximately ¼ mile turn left into Guards Road and then after ¼ mile left into Duns Road. After 200 yards turn right into Home Place for the Ground; From the East: Enter Coldstream via the A6112 or A698 into the High Street then right into Guards Road. Then as above.

CRAIGROYSTON FC

Founded: 1976	**Telephone Nº**: None
Former Names: None	**Fax Number**: None
Nickname: 'Craigie'	**Ground Capacity**: –
Ground: St. Mark's Park, Warriston,	**Seating Capacity**: None
Edinburgh	**Pitch Size**: 108 × 65 yards
Record Attendance: –	**Contact**: Keith Richardson
Colours: Shirts – Yellow	**Contact Phone Nº**: (0131) 538-1453
Shorts – Blue	

PHOTOGRAPH

NOT AVAILABLE

AT TIME OF

GOING TO PRESS

GENERAL INFORMATION
Supporters Club: None
Telephone Nº: –
Car Parking: At the ground
Coach Parking: At the ground
Nearest Railway Station: Edinburgh Waverley
Nearest Bus Station: St. Andrew's Square
Club Shop: None
Opening Times: –
Telephone Nº: –
Postal Sales: –
Nearest Police Station: Ferry Road, Edinburgh
Police Telephone Nº: (0131) 200-7211

ADMISSION INFO (2000/2001 PRICES)
No charge normally. For Scottish Cup games a charge of £2.00 for Adults and £1.00 for Children is made

DISABLED INFORMATION
Wheelchairs: Accommodated
Helpers: –
Prices: –
Disabled Toilets: None
Are Bookings Necessary: No
Contact: –

Travelling Supporters' Information:
Routes: The ground is situated at St. Mark's Park in the Warriston area of Edinburgh.

EASTHOUSES LILY MINERS WELFARE FC

Founded: 1969
Former Names: None
Nickname: 'Houses' 'The Lily'
Ground: Newbattle Complex, Easthouses, Dalkeith
Record Attendance: 550
Colours: Shirts – Red
          Shorts – White

Telephone Nº: (0131) 663-9768
Fax Number: –
Ground Capacity: 1,500
Seating Capacity: None
Pitch Size: 108 × 66 yards
Contact Address: R. Paul, 90 Langlaw Road, Mayfield, Dalkeith EH22 5AS
Contact Phone Nº: (0131) 663-9768

GENERAL INFORMATION

Supporters Club: None
Telephone Nº: –
Car Parking: At the ground
Coach Parking: At the ground
Nearest Railway Station: Dalkeith
Nearest Bus Station: Dalkeith
Club Shop: None
Opening Times: –
Telephone Nº: –
Postal Sales: –
Nearest Police Station: –
Police Telephone Nº: –

GROUND INFORMATION

Away Supporters' Entrances & Sections:
No usual segregation

ADMISSION INFO (2000/2001 PRICES)

No charge normally. For Scottish Cup games a charge of £2.00 for Adults and £1.00 for Children is made

DISABLED INFORMATION

Wheelchairs: Accommodated
Helpers: –
Prices: –
Disabled Toilets: None
Are Bookings Necessary: No
Contact: –

Travelling Supporters' Information:
Routes: From Edinburgh: Follow the A7 through Dalkeith & Newbattle then turn left onto B6482 Bryans Road. Turn right into Easthouses and then take the first left. Take the next right and the ground is at the end of the road.

EDINBURGH ATHLETIC FC

Founded: 1968
Former Names: Manor Thistle FC
Nickname: 'The Crew'
Ground: Muirhouse Sports Ground, Marine Drive, Edinburgh
Record Attendance: Not known
Colours: Shirts – Navy Blue
Shorts – Navy Blue

Telephone Nº: (0131) 332-0650
Fax Number: None
Ground Capacity: 500 approximately
Seating Capacity: None
Pitch Size: 100 × 60 yards
Contact Address: Mr. I Gracie, 1 The Glebe, East Saltoun, East Lothian
Contact Phone Nº: (01875) 340983

GENERAL INFORMATION

Supporters Club: None
Telephone Nº: –
Car Parking: At the ground
Coach Parking: At the ground
Nearest Railway Station: Edinburgh Waverley
Nearest Bus Station: St. Andrew's Square
Club Shop: None
Opening Times: –
Telephone Nº: –
Postal Sales: –
Nearest Police Station: Ferry Road, Edinburgh
Police Telephone Nº: (0131) 200-7211

ADMISSION INFO (2000/2001 PRICES)

No charge normally. For Scottish Cup games a charge of £2.00 for Adults and £1.00 for Children is made
Programme Price: 50p

DISABLED INFORMATION

Wheelchairs: Accommodated
Helpers: –
Prices: –
Disabled Toilets: None
Are Bookings Necessary: No
Contact: –

Travelling Supporters' Information:
Routes: From the West: Take the A90 Queensferry Road into Edinburgh and continue until reaching the B9085 (Quality Street). Turn left into Quality Street and continue into Cramond Road. After ¼ mile turn right into Lauriston Farm Road. Continue to the roundabout and go left along Silver Knowes Road then into Marine Drive for the Ground; From the East: Take the A1 into Edinburgh and at the 1st roundabout take the 2nd exit into Milton Link. At the next roundabout (¼ mile) take 2nd exit onto A199 Sir Harry Lauder Road. Continue along A199 for approximately 2½ miles past Leith then join the A901 (Lindsay Road). Continue along A901 to the end of Lower Granton Road then take the 3rd exit at the roundabout into West Granton Road and after 1¼ mile take the 3rd exit at the roundabout into Marine Drive.

EDINBURGH CITY FC

Founded: 1928 (re-formed 1986)
Former Names: None
Nickname: 'The City'
Ground: Meadowbank Stadium, London Road, Edinburgh   EH7 6AE
Record Attendance: 5,740 (1936)
Colours: Shirts – White
           Shorts – Black

Telephone Nº: (0131) 661-5351
Fax Number: (0131) 652-1633
Ground Capacity: 13,841
Seating Capacity: 13,841
Pitch Size: 105 × 72 yards
Contact Address: D. Baxter, 23 South Elixa Place, Edinburgh   EH8 7PG
Contact Phone Nº: (0131) 652-1633 (home);   (0131) 244-6577 (business)

UNCOVERED SEATING

GENERAL INFORMATION

Social Club: 7/8 Baxter's Place, Edinburgh, EH1 3AF
Telephone Nº: (0131) 557-3838
Car Parking: At the Stadium
Coach Parking: At the Stadium
Nearest Railway Station: Edinburgh Waverley (1 mile)
Nearest Bus Station: St. Andrew's Square (1 mile)
Club Shop: Within the Grandstand
Opening Times: Matchdays from 1 hour before kick-off
Telephone Nº: (0131) 228-1882
Postal Sales: c/o David Beecroft, 19b West Pilton Drive, Edinburgh   EH4 4HR
Nearest Police Station: Portobello, Edinburgh
Police Telephone Nº: (0131) 669-0581

GROUND INFORMATION

Away Supporters' Entrances & Sections:
No usual segregation

ADMISSION INFO (2000/2001 PRICES)
Adult Seating: £3.00
Child Seating: £1.00
Programme Price: £1.00

DISABLED INFORMATION
Wheelchairs: Accommodated on trackside
Helpers: Admitted
Prices: Disabled are charged concessionary prices
Disabled Toilets: Available within the Grandstand
Are Bookings Necessary: No
Contact: (0131) 652-1633 (Secretary)

Travelling Supporters' Information:
Routes: From the West: Leave the M8 at Junction 1 following signs for City Bypass (North). At Gogar roundabout, exit right onto the A8. Head towards the City Centre on the A8 then follow signs for Berwick (A1). Meadowbank stadium is one mile on the left; From the North: Leave the M9 at Junction 1 (Newbridge). Exit left onto the A8 then as from West; From the South: Follow the A1 towards the City Centre. Meadowbank stadium is on the right, one mile before the City Centre.

EDINBURGH UNIVERSITY FC

Founded: 1878
Former Names: None
Nickname: 'The Burgh'
Ground: Peffermill Playing Fields, Peffermill Road, Edinburgh
Record Attendance: Not known
Colours: Shirts – Green
          Shorts – Blue

Telephone Nº: (0131) 667-7541
Fax Number: (0131) 557-4172
Ground Capacity: 212
Seating Capacity: 12
Pitch Size: 115 × 66 yards
Contact Address: C. Hewitt, Edinburgh Univeristy Sports Union, 48 Pleasance, Edinburgh   EH8 9TJ
Contact Phone Nº: (0131) 650-2346/2347

PHOTOGRAPH

NOT AVAILABLE

AT TIME OF

GOING TO PRESS

CLUB HOUSE   CAR PARK

SEATING CABIN

GENERAL INFORMATION
Supporters Club: None
Telephone Nº: –
Car Parking: Spaces for 30 cars at the ground
Coach Parking: None
Nearest Railway Station: Edinburgh Waverley
Nearest Bus Station: St. Andrew Square
Club Shop: None
Opening Times: –
Telephone Nº: –
Postal Sales: –
Nearest Police Station: St. Leonards
Police Telephone Nº: (0131) 662-5000

GROUND INFORMATION
Away Supporters' Entrances & Sections:
No usual segregation

ADMISSION INFO (2000/2001 PRICES)
No charge normally. For Scottish Cup games a charge of £2.00 for Adults and £1.00 for Children is made

DISABLED INFORMATION
Wheelchairs: Accommodated
Helpers: –
Prices: –
Disabled Toilets: None
Are Bookings Necessary: No
Contact: –

Travelling Supporters' Information:
Routes: Peffermill Road is the A6095 which can be reached from the A720 City Bypass. The ground is near the Cameron Toll Shopping Centre.

EYEMOUTH UNITED FC

Founded: 1948	**Colours**: Shirts – Maroon
Former Names: None	Shorts – White
Nickname: 'The Fishermen'	**Telephone N°**: None
Ground: Gunsgreen Park, Johns Road,	**Fax Number**: None
Eyemouth, Berwickshire	**Ground Capacity**: 1,000
Record Attendance: Not known	**Seating Capacity**: None
	Pitch Size: 110 × 70 yards

GENERAL INFORMATION

Supporters Club: None
Telephone N°: –
Car Parking: At the ground
Coach Parking: At the ground
Nearest Railway Station: Berwick-upon-Tweed
Nearest Bus Station: Berwick-upon-Tweed
Club Shop: None
Opening Times: –
Telephone N°: –
Postal Sales: –
Nearest Police Station: Eyemouth
Police Telephone N°: –

ADMISSION INFO (2000/2001 PRICES)

No charge normally. For Scottish Cup games a charge of £2.00 for Adults and £1.00 for Children is made

DISABLED INFORMATION

Wheelchairs: Accommodated
Helpers: –
Prices: –
Disabled Toilets: None
Are Bookings Necessary: No
Contact: –

Travelling Supporters' Information:
Routes: Take the A1107 to Eyemouth. Turn into 'The Avenue' (near the river) and continue along for ½ mile into Johns Road for the ground.

GALA FAIRYDEAN FC

Founded: 1907	**Fax Number:** (01896) 757749
Former Names: None	**Ground Capacity:** 5,500
Nickname: 'The Dean'	**Seating Capacity:** 495
Ground: Netherdale, Galashiels	**Pitch Size:** 110 × 72 yards
Record Attendance: 6,000 (1989)	**Contact Address:** George McGill,
Colours: Shirts – Black and White	25 Melrose Road, Galashiels TD1 2AT
Shorts – Black and White	**Contact Phone Nº:** (01896) 754500;
Telephone Nº: (01896) 753554	Mobile (0831) 575825

GENERAL INFORMATION

Supporters Club: None
Telephone Nº: –
Car Parking: Available at the ground
Coach Parking: Available at the ground
Nearest Railway Station: Edinburgh
Nearest Bus Station: Galashiels
Club Shop: None
Opening Times: –
Telephone Nº: –
Postal Sales: –
Nearest Police Station: Galashiels
Police Telephone Nº: (01896) 752222

GROUND INFORMATION

Away Supporters' Entrances & Sections:
No usual segregation

ADMISSION INFO (2000/2001 PRICES)

Adult Standing: £3.00
Adult Seating: £4.00
Child Standing: Free of charge
Child Seating: £1.00
Programme Price: £1.00

DISABLED INFORMATION

Wheelchairs: Accommodated
Helpers: Please phone the club for details
Prices: Please phone the club for details
Disabled Toilets: None
Are Bookings Necessary: No
Contact: –

Travelling Supporters' Information:
Routes: From Edinburgh: Take the A7 to Galashiels and follow signs for Heriot-Watt University and Netherdale. After passing the Fire Station on left, turn-off left at the mini-roundabout along Tweed Road and the ground is ½ mile on the left; From Jedburgh/Hawick: Take A7 to Galashiels and turn right at mini-roundabout for ground.

HAWICK ROYAL ALBERT FC

Founded: 1947
Former Names: None
Nickname: 'The Albert'
Ground: Albert Park, Mansfield Road, Hawick
Record Attendance: 3,000
Colours: Shirts – Royal Blue
Shorts – Royal Blue

Telephone Nº: (01450) 374231
Fax Number: None
Ground Capacity: 2,000
Seating Capacity: 500
Pitch Size: 100 × 68 yards
Contact Address: J. Batten, 34B Chay Blyth Place, Hawick   TD9 8HY
Contact Phone Nº: (01450) 377447

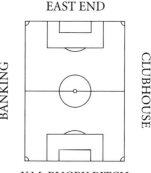

EAST END

BANKING

CLUBHOUSE

Y.M. RUGBY PITCH

GENERAL INFORMATION
Supporters Club: None
Telephone Nº: –
Car Parking: Available at the ground
Coach Parking: Available at the ground
Nearest Railway Station: Edinburgh or Carlisle
Nearest Bus Station: Hawick Centre
Club Shop: None
Opening Times: –
Telephone Nº: –
Postal Sales: –
Nearest Police Station: Wilton Hill, Hawick
Police Telephone Nº: (01450) 375051

GROUND INFORMATION
Away Supporters' Entrances & Sections:
No usual segregation

ADMISSION INFO (1999/2000 PRICES)
Adult Standing: £3.00
Adult Seating: £3.00
Child Standing: £1.00
Child Seating: £1.00
Programme Price: None

DISABLED INFORMATION
Wheelchairs: Accommodated
Helpers: Admitted
Prices: Free of charge for the disabled
Disabled Toilets: None
Are Bookings Necessary: No
Contact: –

Travelling Supporters' Information:
Routes: From the North: Take the A7 into Hawick. At the first set of traffic lights, turn left into Mansfield Road. Follow the river to the roundabout and take the 2nd exit. Albert Park is the third pitch, after the two Rugby pitches on the left; From the South: Take the A7 into Hawick and turn right into Mansfield Road, then as above.

HERIOT-WATT UNIVERSITY FC

Founded: 1942
Former Names: None
Nickname: 'The Watt'
Ground: Heriot-Watt University
Riccarton Campus, Riccarton, Edinburgh
Record Attendance: Not known
Colours: Shirts – Blue and Yellow
Shorts – Blue

Telephone Nº: (0131) 449-5111
Fax Number: None
Ground Capacity: 1,800
Seating Capacity: None
Pitch Size: 116 × 79 yards
Contact Address: R. Silander,
13 Craiglockhart Grove, Edinburgh
EH14 1ET
Contact Phone Nº: (0131) 443-1913

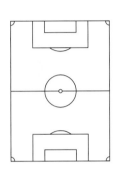

GENERAL INFORMATION
Supporters Club: None
Telephone Nº: –
Car Parking: Available at the ground
Coach Parking: Available at the ground
Nearest Railway Station: Haymarket (5 miles)
Nearest Bus Station: St. Andrews Square (7 miles)
Club Shop: Contact the club for merchandise
Opening Times: –
Telephone Nº: –
Postal Sales: –
Nearest Police Station: Currie
Police Telephone Nº: –

GROUND INFORMATION
Away Supporters' Entrances & Sections:
No usual segregation

ADMISSION INFO (2000/2001 PRICES)
No charge normally. For Scottish Cup games a
charge of £2.00 for Adults and £1.00 for Children is
made
Programme Price: 50p

DISABLED INFORMATION
Wheelchairs: Accommodated
Helpers: Admitted
Prices: Free of charge
Disabled Toilets: Available
Are Bookings Necessary: No
Contact: (0131) 449-511

Web site: www.cee.hw.ac.uk/~ceercs/hwufc

Travelling Supporters' Information:
Routes: From the South: Take the Edinburgh City Bypass west and follow signs for the University. Ground is on
the University Campus; From the West: Take the Edinburgh City Bypass east and follow signs for the University.

KELSO UNITED FC

Founded: 1924	**Telephone N°:** (01573) 223780
Former Names: None	**Fax Number:** None
Nickname: 'Tweedsiders'	**Ground Capacity:** 1,000
Ground: Woodside Park, Kelso,	**Seating Capacity:** None
Roxburghshire	**Pitch Size:** 100 × 66 yards
Record Attendance: 700	**Contact Address:** A.H. Douglas,
Colours: Shirts – Black and White stripes	34 Dyers Court, Kelso TD5 7NQ
Shorts – Black	**Contact Phone N°:** (01573) 225314

CLUBHOUSE

GENERAL INFORMATION

Supporters Club: None
Telephone N°: –
Car Parking: At the ground
Coach Parking: At the ground
Nearest Railway Station: Berwick-upon-Tweed (25 miles)
Nearest Bus Station: Kelso (½ mile)
Club Shop: None
Opening Times: –
Telephone N°: –
Postal Sales: –
Nearest Police Station: Kelso (½ mile)
Police Telephone N°: (01573) 223434

ADMISSION INFO (2000/2001 PRICES)

No charge normally. For Scottish Cup games a charge of £2.00 for Adults and £1.00 for Children is made

DISABLED INFORMATION

Wheelchairs: Accommodated
Helpers: –
Prices: –
Disabled Toilets: Available
Are Bookings Necessary: No
Contact: –

Travelling Supporters' Information:
Routes: From Selkirk on A699: Enter Kelso and turn left over the bridge. Go straight on into the Town Square then turn right next to the Bank. Go straight on at the first mini-roundabout then turn left at the next mini-roundabout. Woodside Park is on the right, before the roundabout; From Edinburgh on A6089: Follow signs to the racecourse. Pass the racecourse on the left, continue to the end of the road then turn right. At the mini-roundabout go straight on. Woodside Park is on the left.

LOTHIAN THISTLE FC

Founded: 1969
Former Names: None
Nickname: 'Thistle'
Ground: Saughton Sports Complex, Edinburgh
Record Attendance: Not known
Colours: Shirts – Maroon
    Shorts – Sky Blue

Phone N°: (0131) 444-0422 (matchdays)
Fax Number: (0131) 333-3900
Ground Capacity: 1,000
Seating Capacity: None
Pitch Size: 112 × 74 yards
Contact Address: Tom Allison, 31 Clermiston Place, Edinburgh EH4 7DN
Contact Phone N°: (0131) 336-1751 (home); (0131) 333-1976 (business)

GENERAL INFORMATION
Supporters Club: None
Telephone N°: –
Car Parking: At the ground
Coach Parking: At the ground
Nearest Railway Station: Edinburgh Haymarket (2 miles)
Nearest Bus Station: St. Andrew's Square
Club Shop: None
Opening Times: –
Telephone N°: –
Postal Sales: –
Nearest Police Station: Edinburgh
Police Telephone N°: (0131) 334-4900

ADMISSION INFO (2000/2001 PRICES)
Adult Standing: £2.00
Child Standing: £1.00
Programme Price: Included with admission cost

DISABLED INFORMATION
Wheelchairs: Accommodated
Helpers: –
Prices: –
Disabled Toilets: None
Are Bookings Necessary: No
Contact: –

Travelling Supporters' Information:
Routes: The ground is situated approximately ½ mile from Tynecastle Park. See Hearts information (page 77) for detailed directions and follow signs for Saughton Sports Complex.

PEEBLES ROVERS FC

Founded: 1894	**Colours:** Shirts – Red and White
Former Names: None	Shorts – Red and White
Nickname: 'The Rovers'	**Telephone Nº:** None
Ground: Whitestone Park, Peebles	**Fax Number:** –
Record Attendance: Not known	**Ground Capacity:** 3,000
Pitch Size: 110 × 70 yards	**Seating Capacity:** 500

STAND

GENERAL INFORMATION
Supporters Club: None
Telephone Nº: –
Car Parking: At the ground
Coach Parking: At the ground
Nearest Railway Station: Carstairs Junction
Nearest Bus Station: Peebles
Club Shop: None
Opening Times: –
Telephone Nº: –
Postal Sales: –
Nearest Police Station: Peebles
Police Telephone Nº: –

ADMISSION INFO (2000/2001 PRICES)
Adult Standing: £2.00
Adult Seating: £2.00
Child Standing: £2.00
Child Seating: £2.00
Programme Price: –

DISABLED INFORMATION
Wheelchairs: Accommodated
Helpers: Please phone the club for details
Prices: Please phone the club for details
Disabled Toilets: None
Are Bookings Necessary: No
Contact: –

Travelling Supporters' Information:
Routes: The ground is situated next to the Leisure Centre on the A72 main road through Peebles.

PENCAITLAND & ORMISTON FC

Founded: 1884
Former Names: Pencaitland Amateur FC, Pencaitland FC & Ormiston Primrose FC
Nickname: None
Ground: Recreation Park, Ormiston, East Lothian
Record Attendance: Unknown
Colours: Shirts – Maroon and White
Shorts – Maroon

Telephone Nº: None
Ground Capacity: 1,000
Seating Capacity: None
Pitch Size: 108 × 68 yards
Contact Address: T. Weir, 103 Moffat Road, Ormiston, East Lothian
Contact Phone Nº: (01875) 611322

GENERAL INFORMATION

Supporters Club: None
Telephone Nº: –
Car Parking: Available at the ground
Coach Parking: None
Nearest Railway Station: Edinburgh Waverley
Nearest Bus Station: Edinburgh
Club Shop: None
Opening Times: –
Telephone Nº: –
Postal Sales: –
Nearest Police Station: Tranent
Police Telephone Nº: (01875) 610333

GROUND INFORMATION

Away Supporters' Entrances & Sections:
No usual segregation

ADMISSION INFO (2000/2001 PRICES)

Adult Standing: £2.00
Child Standing: £1.00
Programme Price: 50p

DISABLED INFORMATION

Wheelchairs: Accommodated
Helpers: Please phone the club for details
Prices: Please phone the club for details
Disabled Toilets: None
Are Bookings Necessary: No
Contact: –

Travelling Supporters' Information:
Routes: Head East from Dalkeith on the A68 then take the A6093 towards Pencaitland. Turn left onto B6371 into Ormiston. At the bend in the road before entering Ormiston Village turn left opposite the Primary School and then first left again. The ground is situated on the left.

PRESTON ATHLETIC FC

Founded: 1945
Former Names: None
Nickname: 'Panners'
Ground: Pennypit Park, Rope Walk, Prestonpans, East Lothian
Record Attendance: Unknown
Pitch Size: 110 × 72 yards

Colours: Shirts – Navy Blue with Red and White trim
 Shorts – Navy Blue
Telephone Nº: None
Fax Number: None
Ground Capacity: 4,000
Seating Capacity: 313

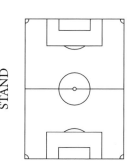

GENERAL INFORMATION

Supporters Club: None
Telephone Nº: –
Car Parking: At the ground
Coach Parking: At the ground
Nearest Railway Station: Musselburgh
Nearest Bus Station: St. Andrew's Square, Edinburgh
Club Shop: None
Opening Times: –
Telephone Nº: –
Postal Sales: –
Nearest Police Station: Edinburgh
Police Telephone Nº: (0131) 344-4900

GROUND INFORMATION

Away Supporters' Entrances & Sections:
No usual segregation

ADMISSION INFO (2000/2001 PRICES)

No charge normally. For Scottish Cup games a charge of £2.00 for Adults and £1.00 for Children is made
Programme Price: £1.00

DISABLED INFORMATION

Wheelchairs: Accommodated
Helpers: Please phone the club for details
Prices: Please phone the club for details
Disabled Toilets: None
Are Bookings Necessary: No
Contact: –

Travelling Supporters' Information:
Routes: Take the A198 to Prestonpans. Upon reaching Prestonpans, take the B1361 into town turn into West Loan then left again at the end of the road into High Street. Turn left by the chip shop into Redburn Road then left again into Rope Walk for the ground.

SELKIRK FC

Founded: 1880
Former Names: None
Nickname: 'Souters'
Ground: Ettrick Park, Riverside Road, Selkirk, Selkirkshire
Record Attendance: 3,000
Colours: Shirts – Royal Blue with White trim
Shorts – Royal Blue with White trim

Telephone Nº: (01750) 20478
Fax Number: None
Ground Capacity: 3,000
Seating Capacity: None
Pitch Size: 108 × 70 yards
Contact Address: D. Kerr, 17 Kilncroft, Selkirk
Contact Phone Nº: (01750) 23060

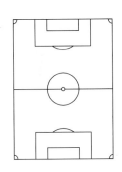

GENERAL INFORMATION

Supporters Club: None
Telephone Nº: –
Car Parking: Available at the ground
Coach Parking: Available at the ground
Nearest Railway Station: Edinburgh
Nearest Bus Station: Selkirk
Club Shop: None
Opening Times: –
Telephone Nº: –
Postal Sales: –
Nearest Police Station: Selkirk
Police Telephone Nº: –

GROUND INFORMATION

Away Supporters' Entrances & Sections:
No usual segregation

ADMISSION INFO (2000/2001 PRICES)

Adult Standing: £2.00
Child Standing: £1.00
Programme Price: –

DISABLED INFORMATION

Wheelchairs: Accommodated
Helpers: Please phone the club for details
Prices: Please phone the club for details
Disabled Toilets: None
Are Bookings Necessary: No
Contact: –

Travelling Supporters' Information:
Routes: From Edinburgh: Take the A7 to Selkirk. Turn right by the Monument in the market place and follow the road towards the river. Before the bridge turn right into Buccleuch Road. Continue as far as North Riverside Industrial Area and turn left into the Industrial Area. The ground is next to St. Mary's Mill; From Hawick: Take the A7 into Selkirk and turn left by the Monument. Then as from Edinburgh.

THE SPARTANS FC

Founded: 1951
Former Names: None
Nickname: None
Ground: City Park, Ferry Road, Edinburgh
Record Attendance: –
Colours: Shirts – White
Shorts – Red

Telephone Nº: None
Fax Number: –
Ground Capacity: 3,000
Seating Capacity: –
Pitch Size: 108 × 65 yards
Contact Address: J. Murray, 60 Ratcliffe Terrace, Edinburgh   EH9 1QU
Contact Phone Nº: (0131) 668-2188 (home);   (0131) 667-9923 (business)

GENERAL INFORMATION
Supporters Club: None
Telephone Nº: –
Car Parking: At the ground
Coach Parking: Adjacent to the ground
Nearest Railway Station: Edinburgh Waverley
Nearest Bus Station: St. Andrew's Square
Club Shop: None
Opening Times: –
Telephone Nº: –
Postal Sales: –
Nearest Police Station: Ferry Road, Edinburgh
Police Telephone Nº: (0131) 200-7211

ADMISSION INFO (2000/2001 PRICES)
Adult Standing: £3.00
Child Standing: £1.50
Programme Price: –

DISABLED INFORMATION
Wheelchairs: Accommodated
Helpers: Please phone the club for details
Prices: Please phone the club for details
Disabled Toilets: None
Are Bookings Necessary: No
Contact: –

Travelling Supporters' Information:
Routes: From the West: Take the A90 Queensferry Road into Edinburgh and continue until reaching the A902 (Telford Road). Turn left into Telford Road and take the 3rd exit at the roundabout into Ferry Road for the ground; From the East: Take the A1 into Edinburgh and at the 1st roundabout take the 2nd exit into Milton Link. At the next roundabout (¼ mile) take 2nd exit onto A199 Sir Harry Lauder Road. Continue along A199 for approximately 2½ miles past Leith then turn left onto the A902 which continues into Ferry Road for the ground.

THREAVE ROVERS FC

Founded: 1953
Former Names: None
Nickname: 'Rovers'
Ground: Meadow Park, Castle Douglas, Dumfries & Galloway
Record Attendance: 2,000
Colours: Shirts – Black and White stripes
Shorts – Black

Telephone Nº: (01556) 504536
Fax Number: (01556) 503512
Ground Capacity: 1,500
Seating Capacity: None
Pitch Size: 110 × 80 yards
Contact Address: Bobby McCleary, 298 King Street, Castle Douglas DG7 1HA
Contact Phone Nº: (01556) 503512

GENERAL INFORMATION
Supporters Club: Yes
Telephone Nº: (01556) 503667
Car Parking: Available at the ground
Coach Parking: None
Nearest Railway Station: Dumfries (18 miles)
Nearest Bus Station: Castle Douglas
Club Shop: At the ground
Opening Times: Matchdays only
Telephone Nº: –
Postal Sales: –
Nearest Police Station: Castle Douglas
Police Telephone Nº: (01556) 502277

GROUND INFORMATION
Away Supporters' Entrances & Sections:
No usual segregation

ADMISSION INFO (2000/2001 PRICES)
Adult Standing: £3.00
Child Standing: £1.50
Senior Citizen Standing: £1.50
Programme Price: Free of charge

DISABLED INFORMATION
Wheelchairs: Accommodated
Helpers: Please phone the club for details
Prices: Please phone the club for details
Disabled Toilets: Available
Are Bookings Necessary: No
Contact: –

Travelling Supporters' Information:
Routes: Take the A75 to Castle Douglas. Pass along King Street and turn right into Marle Street (by the Chip shop). The ground is situated about 100 yards on the left.

TOLLCROSS UNITED FC

Founded: 1971
Former Names: None
Nickname: 'The Cross'
Ground: Fernieside Recreation Park, Fernieside Avenue, Edinburgh
Record Attendance: 400
Colours: Shirts – Red with White sleeves
Shorts – White
Pitch Size: 115 × 76 yards

Telephone Nº: (0589) 931054 – Mobile (Matchdays only)
Fax Number: (0131) 467-5535
Ground Capacity: 400
Seating Capacity: None
Contact Address: Alistair Wilkie, 3/1 Rankin Avenue, Edinburgh EH9 3DD
Contact Phone Nº: (0131) 621-1148 (home); (0131) 467-5555 (business)

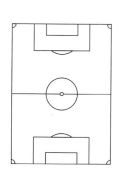

GENERAL INFORMATION

Supporters Club: None
Telephone Nº: –
Car Parking: At the ground
Coach Parking: At the ground
Nearest Railway Station: Edinburgh Waverley
Nearest Bus Station: St. Andrew's Square
Club Shop: None
Opening Times: –
Telephone Nº: –
Postal Sales: –
Nearest Police Station: Edinburgh
Police Telephone Nº: (0131) 669-0581

GROUND INFORMATION

Away Supporters' Entrances & Sections:
No usual segregation

ADMISSION INFO (2000/2001 PRICES)

Adult Standing: £4.00
Child Standing: £2.00
Programme Price: 50p

DISABLED INFORMATION

Wheelchairs: Accommodated
Helpers: –
Prices: Please phone the club for details
Disabled Toilets: None
Are Bookings Necessary: No
Contact: –

Travelling Supporters' Information:
Routes: The ground is situated on the A7 Edinburgh to Dalkeith road near to the New Royal Infirmary.

VALE OF LEITHEN FC

Founded: 1891	**Telephone Nº:** None
Former Names: None	**Fax Number:** None
Nickname: 'Vale'	**Ground Capacity:** 1,500
Ground: Victoria Park, Innerleithen	**Seating Capacity:** None
Record Attendance: 3,500	**Pitch Size:** 108 × 70 yards
Colours: Shirts – Navy with White sleeves	**Contact Address:** I. Haggarty, 11 Peebles
Shorts – Navy	Road, Innerleithen EH44 6QX
	Contact Phone Nº: (01896) 830995
	(home); (0131) 244-2524 (business)

GENERAL INFORMATION
Supporters Club: None
Telephone Nº: –
Car Parking: Available at the ground
Coach Parking: Available at the ground
Nearest Railway Station: Edinburgh
Nearest Bus Station: Peebles
Club Shop: None
Opening Times: –
Telephone Nº: –
Postal Sales: –
Nearest Police Station: Innerleithen
Police Telephone Nº: (01896) 830217

GROUND INFORMATION
Away Supporters' Entrances & Sections:
No usual segregation

ADMISSION INFO (2000/2001 PRICES)
Adult Standing: £2.00
Child Standing: £1.00
Programme Price: 50p

DISABLED INFORMATION
Wheelchairs: Accommodated
Helpers: Please phone the club for details
Prices: Please phone the club for details
Disabled Toilets: Available opposite the ground
Are Bookings Necessary: No
Contact: (01896) 830995 (Secretary)

Travelling Supporters' Information:
Routes: Take the A72 to Innerleithen from Peebles. Upon entering Innerleithen, turn left into Hall Street at the crossroads for access to the ground.

WHITEHILL WELFARE FC

Founded: 1953	**Telephone N°:** (0131) 440-0115
Former Names: None	**Fax Number:** None
Nickname: 'The Welfare'	**Ground Capacity:** 4,000
Ground: Ferguson Park, Carnethie Street, Rosewell, Midlothian	**Seating Capacity:** None
	Pitch Size: 108 × 70 yards
Record Attendance: 2,000 (vs Celtic)	**Contact Address:** Peter McGauley,
Colours: Shirts – Maroon with Sky Blue Shorts – White	47 Prestonhall Crescent, Rosewell, Midlothian EH24 9BQ
	Contact Phone N°: (0131) 440-3417

 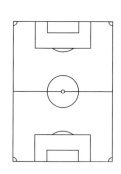

GENERAL INFORMATION
Supporters Club: None
Telephone N°: –
Car Parking: At the ground
Coach Parking: At the ground
Nearest Railway Station: Edinburgh Waverley
Nearest Bus Station: St. Andrew's Square, Edinburgh
Club Shop: None
Opening Times: –
Telephone N°: –
Postal Sales: –
Nearest Police Station: Dalkeith
Police Telephone N°: –

GROUND INFORMATION
Away Supporters' Entrances & Sections:
No usual segregation

ADMISSION INFO (2000/2001 PRICES)
Adult Standing: £3.00
Child Standing: £1.50
Programme Price: –

DISABLED INFORMATION
Wheelchairs: Accommodated
Helpers: Please phone the club for details
Prices: Please phone the club for details
Disabled Toilets: Available
Are Bookings Necessary: No
Contact: –

Travelling Supporters' Information:
Routes: From Edinburgh: Take the A6094 into Rosewell. In Rosewell, turn left then left again opposite St. Matthews Roman Catholic Primary School. The ground is situated next to Ferguson Park Garage.

Scottish League Premier Division 1999/2000	Aberdeen	Celtic	Dundee	Dundee United	Heart of Midlothian	Hibernian	Kilmarnock	Motherwell	Rangers	St. Johnstone
Aberdeen	■	0-5	0-2	1-2	3-1	2-2	2-2	1-1	1-5	0-3
	■	0-6	0-1	3-1	1-2	4-0	5-1	2-1	1-1	2-1
Celtic	7-0	■	6-2	4-1	4-0	4-0	5-1	0-1	1-1	3-0
	5-1	■	2-2	2-0	2-3	1-1	4-2	4-0	0-1	4-1
Dundee	1-3	1-2	■	0-2	1-0	3-4	0-0	0-1	2-3	1-2
	0-2	0-3	■	3-0	0-0	1-0	1-2	4-1	1-7	1-1
Dundee United	3-1	2-1	2-1	■	0-2	3-1	0-0	0-2	0-4	1-0
	1-1	0-1	1-0	■	0-1	0-0	2-2	1-2	0-2	0-1
Heart of Midlothian	3-0	1-2	4-0	3-0	■	0-3	2-2	1-1	0-4	1-1
	3-0	1-0	2-0	1-2	■	2-1	0-0	0-0	1-2	0-0
Hibernian	2-0	0-2	5-2	3-2	1-1	■	0-3	2-2	0-1	0-1
	1-0	2-1	1-2	1-0	3-1	■	2-2	2-2	2-2	3-3
Kilmarnock	2-0	0-1	0-0	1-1	2-2	0-2	■	0-1	1-1	1-2
	1-0	1-1	2-2	1-0	0-1	1-0	■	0-2	0-2	3-2
Motherwell	5-6	3-2	0-2	2-2	2-1	2-2	0-4	■	1-5	1-0
	1-0	1-1	0-3	1-3	0-2	2-0	2-0	■	2-0	2-1
Rangers	3-0	4-2	1-2	4-1	1-0	2-0	2-1	4-1	■	3-1
	5-0	4-0	3-0	3-0	1-0	5-2	1-0	6-2	■	0-0
St. Johnstone	1-1	1-2	0-1	0-1	1-4	1-1	2-0	1-1	1-1	■
	2-1	0-0	2-1	2-0	0-1	1-0	0-0	1-1	0-2	■

Scottish Premier League

Season 1999/2000

Rangers	36	28	6	2	96	26	90
Celtic	36	21	6	9	90	38	69
Heart of Midlothian	36	15	9	12	47	40	54
Motherwell	36	14	10	12	49	63	52
St. Johnstone	36	10	12	14	36	44	42
Hibernian	36	10	11	15	49	61	41
Dundee	36	12	5	19	45	64	41
Dundee United	36	11	6	19	34	57	39
Kilmarnock	36	8	13	15	38	52	37
Aberdeen	36	9	6	21	44	83	33

Champions: Rangers

Scottish League Division One 1999/2000	Airdrieonians	Ayr United	Clydebank	Dunfermline Athletic	Falkirk	Inverness Caledonian	Livingston	Greenock Morton	Raith Rovers	St. Mirren
Airdrieonians	■	2-1	1-0	2-2	0-0	1-1	2-3	1-0	1-4	0-2
	■	0-0	0-0	1-2	0-2	1-4	0-2	3-0	0-2	0-1
Ayr United	2-0	■	0-0	0-3	1-1	1-0	1-2	3-0	0-1	0-3
	5-0	■	4-0	0-2	3-3	1-3	0-1	3-2	0-1	1-2
Clydebank	0-2	0-2	■	1-4	0-3	0-3	1-5	1-3	1-1	2-3
	1-1	0-2	■	1-3	0-1	0-1	1-2	0-3	2-1	0-0
Dunfermline Athletic	0-0	2-1	2-1	■	1-1	4-0	3-0	2-1	1-1	1-1
	1-0	2-0	6-0	■	2-2	1-0	4-1	1-1	0-2	1-1
Falkirk	2-0	2-1	3-2	1-3	■	0-2	0-2	2-4	2-1	3-1
	8-0	1-0	4-0	1-1	■	2-2	2-3	2-1	1-0	2-0
Inverness Caledonian Thistle	2-0	1-1	1-0	1-1	2-3	■	2-0	1-1	0-2	1-1
	1-5	1-1	4-1	1-2	0-3	■	4-1	6-2	1-1	5-0
Livingston	3-0	4-1	2-1	0-1	1-1	2-2	■	2-1	1-1	1-2
	3-2	3-1	3-0	1-0	0-1	1-1	■	1-0	0-0	1-2
Greenock Morton	0-2	0-0	0-0	0-3	2-3	5-1	2-2	■	2-0	1-4
	4-0	1-2	1-0	2-0	0-2	0-2	1-0	■	1-0	0-2
Raith Rovers	1-1	5-1	1-0	2-2	2-1	4-2	3-1	3-1	■	0-6
	2-0	2-0	0-0	3-0	0-1	2-0	1-3	3-0	■	1-2
St. Mirren	5-0	1-1	2-1	3-1	2-1	3-2	1-1	3-2	3-2	■
	3-1	1-2	8-0	0-2	1-0	2-0	0-2	1-1	3-0	■

Scottish League Division One

Season 1999/2000

St. Mirren	36	23	7	6	75	39	76
Dunfermline Athletic	36	20	11	5	66	33	71
Falkirk	36	20	8	8	67	40	68
Livingston	36	19	7	10	60	45	64
Raith Rovers	36	17	8	11	55	40	59
Inverness Caledonian Thistle	36	13	10	13	60	55	49
Ayr United	36	10	8	18	42	52	38
Greenock Morton	36	10	6	20	45	61	36
Airdrieonians	36	7	8	21	29	69	29
Clydebank	36	1	7	28	17	82	10

Promoted: St. Mirren and Dunfermline Athletic

Relegated: Clydebank

Scottish League Division Two 1999/2000	Alloa Athletic	Arbroath	Clyde	Hamilton Academical	Partick Thistle	Queen of the South	Ross County	Stenhousemuir	Stirling Albion	Stranraer
Alloa Athletic		0-0	1-0	1-1	1-0	3-1	2-0	1-4	4-4	1-1
		2-1	2-1	2-0	1-1	6-1	1-2	3-1	1-0	4-0
Arbroath	2-2		2-1	1-1	0-0	5-2	0-1	0-3	2-1	1-2
	2-0		1-1	1-1	3-2	1-2	1-2	2-2	3-2	1-1
Clyde	0-1	0-0		2-1	2-0	3-0	3-1	1-0	3-0	0-0
	0-0	4-1		1-0	1-0	3-1	0-0	7-0	4-1	1-1
Hamilton Academical	1-2	2-2	2-3		0-0	0-3	1-0	1-1	0-2	2-1
	0-0	2-2	1-1		0-1	1-1	0-3	2-1	1-0	2-0
Partick Thistle	2-2	1-3	0-0	0-1		2-0	0-2	0-1	1-0	2-0
	0-1	2-0	1-2	2-2		5-4	4-2	1-0	1-1	1-1
Queen of the South	1-1	2-3	1-1	3-2	1-2		0-2	0-3	3-3	0-5
	2-1	1-0	3-0	1-1	1-1		0-3	3-1	2-3	0-0
Ross County	1-0	2-0	2-0	2-1	2-1	1-1		0-0	1-3	1-1
	3-4	1-1	2-2	0-1	1-3	2-0		2-0	5-1	3-1
Stenhousemuir	1-3	1-3	1-3	0-0	0-1	2-1	0-2		2-1	1-1
	2-1	3-0	3-4	0-1	2-0	2-0	2-2		1-2	1-1
Stirling Albion	0-1	3-4	1-2	2-0	3-1	3-0	2-1	5-1		1-1
	1-1	1-1	3-6	1-4	0-2	2-2	3-1	1-0		2-5
Stranraer	0-0	2-2	2-2	0-2	1-1	1-0	0-0	2-0	2-1	
	2-2	0-1	2-1	2-2	3-1	1-2	0-2	2-2	3-1	

Scottish League Division Two

Season 1999/2000

Clyde	36	18	11	7	65	37	65
Alloa Athletic	36	17	13	6	58	38	64
Ross County	36	18	8	10	57	39	62
Arbroath	36	11	14	11	52	55	47
Partick Thistle	36	12	10	14	42	44	46
Stranraer	36	9	18	9	47	46	45
Stirling Albion	36	11	7	18	60	72	40
Stenhousemuir	36	10	8	18	44	59	38
Queen of the South	36	8	9	19	45	75	33
* Hamilton Academical	36	10	14	12	39	44	29

* Hamilton Academical had 15 points deducted

Promoted: Clyde, Alloa Athletic and Ross County

Relegated: Hamilton Academical

89

Scottish League Division Three 1999/2000	Albion Rovers	Berwick Rangers	Brechin City	Cowdenbeath	Dumbarton	East Fife	East Stirlingshire	Forfar Athletic	Montrose	Queen's Park
Albion Rovers		0-3	0-0	1-4	1-3	1-3	1-1	0-1	1-3	2-4
		0-0	0-2	0-3	3-0	3-1	0-1	0-1	0-2	0-3
Berwick Rangers	1-1		2-0	0-2	0-1	0-1	1-0	2-2	0-0	1-2
	2-1		3-1	0-0	0-0	0-1	3 0	2 0	2-1	1-1
Brechin City	8-1	0-3		2-0	0-2	1-3	1-2	0-2	1-0	1-2
	3-2	1-2		1-2	1-2	3-1	1-1	1-0	0-0	0-0
Cowdenbeath	0-0	1-1	6-1		0-2	4-0	1-2	0-3	1-1	0-2
	5-0	1-3	1-1		1-2	1-0	0-0	4-1	2-1	2-3
Dumbarton	1-1	2-1	1-3	1-1		1-1	1-0	3-3	3-4	0-1
	0-0	0-2	2-1	2-0		2-1	3-0	0-0	3-2	1-1
East Fife	1-4	1-2	1-0	2-3	1-0		1-0	2-0	0-0	0-0
	2-1	3-1	1-1	1-1	2-1		3-1	1-1	2-0	0-0
East Stirlingshire	4-3	0-3	0-0	0-1	1-3	0-2		0-2	2-0	1-1
	3-1	0-1	0-3	0-4	2-1	1-0		0-1	1-0	0-1
Forfar Athletic	2-0	1-1	0-0	3-1	5-0	3-2	1-1		1-2	2-2
	3-1	2-0	2-0	2-2	4-3	0-1	3-0		1-2	4-0
Montrose	2-1	1-2	0-1	0-1	1-4	1-2	1-2	2-0		2-1
	1-2	2-3	1-0	1-3	2-1	1-1	0-0	1-5		0-2
Queen's Park	2-0	1-4	5-3	1-0	3-2	0-1	2-1	1-1	2-1	
	0-1	0-1	1-0	3-1	2-0	1-0	0-1	3-2	1-1	

Scottish League Division Three

Season 1999/2000

Queen's Park	36	20	9	7	54	37	69
Berwick Rangers	36	19	9	8	53	30	66
Forfar Athletic	36	17	10	9	64	40	61
East Fife	36	17	8	11	45	39	59
Cowdenbeath	36	15	9	12	59	43	54
Dumbarton	36	15	8	13	53	51	53
East Stirlingshire	36	11	7	18	28	50	40
Brechin City	36	10	8	18	42	51	38
Montrose	36	10	7	19	39	54	37
Albion Rovers	36	5	7	24	33	75	22

Promoted: Queen's Park, Berwick Rangers and Forfar Athletic

	Brora Rangers	Buckie Thistle	Clachnacuddin	Cove Rangers	Deveronvale	Elgin City	Forres Mechanics	Fort William	Fraserburgh	Huntly	Keith	Lossiemouth	Nairn County	Peterhead	Rothes	Wick Academy
Brora Rangers		0-2	0-1	2-2	2-5	2-2	0-0	3-2	1-1	1-2	0-1	1-1	3-3	0-1	3-5	6-0
Buckie Thistle	0-1		0-0	2-1	1-1	1-1	1-1	3-0	1-1	2-0	0-2	5-1	3-1	2-0	3-2	3-1
Clachnacuddin	1-1	1-2		5-1	2-3	0-2	1-2	6-1	0-1	2-4	2-3	1-0	4-0	0-2	1-0	4-2
Cove Rangers	3-1	1-2	2-0		2-2	4-2	4-2	7-1	2-3	0-0	2-3	0-2	7-0	2-3	1-5	9-1
Deveronvale	0-2	1-3	0-2	3-3		2-1	4-3	5-1	3-5	0-4	0-4	1-4	4-0	3-2	2-0	4-2
Elgin City	5-1	0-2	0-2	1-0	1-0		1-2	2-1	1-2	0-0	3-3	3-2	1-1	1-0	1-0	3-1
Forres Mechs.	1-2	2-1	0-5	2-1	4-0	3-0		3-1	3-1	3-2	1-1	1-1	2-1	1-2	4-1	0-1
Fort William	1-6	0-2	2-2	3-3	1-1	1-5	0-6		3-4	1-2	1-4	0-1	2-2	1-2	0-4	2-2
Fraserburgh	4-0	1-1	1-2	0-0	0-0	2-1	2-0	7-1		2-0	7-1	0-0	2-1	3-1	1-1	7-1
Huntly	4-2	2-5	3-2	1-3	4-1	4-2	3-3	3-0	2-3		2-1	2-0	9-0	2-1	1-1	1-1
Keith	3-4	4-2	1-2	3-4	3-0	2-0	3-0	4-0	3-2	2-2		6-1	3-0	1-0	1-0	4-0
Lossiemouth	3-1	2-2	2-4	3-1	0-2	3-2	1-1	6-0	0-3	2-1	0-2		2-1	1-4	0-1	1-1
Nairn County	0-2	0-2	1-1	0-9	1-0	1-1	1-5	1-4	0-4	1-0	1-5	0-5		1-4	1-1	3-2
Peterhead	5-3	2-0	0-0	1-0	4-1	2-1	1-1	6-2	2-2	1-1	0-2	3-4	3-1		1-0	7-2
Rothes	1-4	2-3	0-0	0-1	0-3	1-2	0-1	3-1	0-4	2-4	0-1	4-1	1-1	1-3		2-1
Wick Academy	2-1	0-2	1-2	1-6	3-0	1-0	0-3	2-1	1-1	2-4	2-0	1-2	0-0	0-3	2-3	

Highland Football League

Season 1999/2000

Keith	30	21	3	6	76	38	66
Fraserburgh	30	17	10	3	75	32	61
Buckie Thistle	30	18	7	5	58	31	61
Peterhead	30	18	4	8	66	39	58
Huntly	30	15	7	8	69	46	52
Forres Mechanics	30	15	7	8	60	42	52
Clachnacuddin	30	14	6	10	55	37	48
Cove Rangers	30	12	6	12	81	54	42
Elgin City	30	12	6	12	45	44	42
Lossiemouth	30	12	6	12	52	56	42
Deveronvale	30	11	5	14	51	63	38
Brora Rangers	30	9	6	15	53	61	33
Rothes	30	8	5	17	41	52	29
Wick Academy	30	6	5	19	36	84	23
Nairn County	30	3	8	19	24	91	17
Fort William	30	1	5	24	34	107	8

Champions: Keith

Peterhead and Elgin City were elected as new members of the
Scottish League

East of Scotland League Premier Division 1999/2000	Annan Athletic	Civil Service Stroll.	Coldstream	Craigroyston	Easthouses Lily	Edinburgh City	Lothian Thistle	Peebles Rovers	Spartans	Tollcross United	Vale of Leithen	Whitehill Welfare
Annan Athletic	■	4-3	1-1	2-0	2-1	2-1	2-1	9-1	1-1	2-0	6-3	1-1
Civil Serv. Stroll.	0-4	■	3-1	1-4	2-1	4-2	3-2	0-2	2-2	6-0	0-3	2-1
Coldstream	0-4	5-1	■	2-0	7-1	1-1	1-1	1-2	1-3	4-1	1-1	0-1
Craigroyston	0-1	0-2	2-1	■	2-0	1-4	2-4	1-0	0-4	3-2	5-2	0-10
Easthouses Lily	1-4	2-1	0-1	0-1	■	2-2	2-0	2-0	0-1	2-0	0-1	1-1
Edinburgh City	1-1	3-1	0-3	2-1	2-0	■	2-1	1-0	4-1	4-1	3-3	0-2
Lothian Thistle	2-0	3-3	1-2	2-0	4-1	2-1	■	4-2	2-2	5-0	2-2	0-2
Peebles Rovers	0-3	2-1	2-1	3-3	2-3	2-4	1-2	■	0-4	4-0	0-2	0-2
Spartans	1-1	2-1	6-0	5-2	6-1	3-1	2-1	5-1	■	5-1	2-1	1-1
Tollcross United	0-5	1-2	1-0	0-2	2-4	3-3	1-2	2-3	2-5	■	0-1	0-3
Vale of Leithen	1-5	2-3	4-1	4-0	4-2	2-0	1-3	4-1	5-0	4-2	■	0-4
Whitehill Welfare	2-1	1-1	4-0	2-0	5-1	3-1	0-1	2-1	3-1	7-0	2-0	■

East of Scotland League

Premier Division Season 1999/2000

Annan Athletic	22	15	6	1	62	21	51
Whitehill Welfare	22	15	5	2	59	13	50
Spartans	22	14	5	3	62	31	47
Lothian Thistle	22	11	4	7	45	32	37
Vale of Leithen	22	11	3	8	50	42	36
Edinburgh City	22	9	5	8	42	39	32
Civil Service Strollers	22	9	3	10	42	47	30
Coldstream	22	7	4	11	34	40	25
Craigroyston	22	8	1	13	29	53	25
Easthouses Lily	22	6	2	14	27	50	20
Peebles Rovers	22	6	1	15	29	56	19
Tollcross United	22	1	1	20	19	76	4

Champions: Annan Athletic

Relegated: Tollcross United and Peebles Rovers

East of Scotland League First Division 1999/2000	Edinburgh Athletic	Edinburgh Univ.	Eyemouth United	Gala Fairydean	Hawick Royal Alb.	Heriot-Watt Univ.	Kelso United	Pencait. & Ormiston	Preston Athletic	Selkirk	Threave Rovers
Edinburgh Ath.	■	1-0	0-1	0-1	1-0	2-0	1-2	0-2	2-5	3-2	1-4
Edinburgh Univ.	4-1	■	2-0	1-0	1-2	3-2	2-2	0-2	0-3	5-0	1-2
Eyemouth United	4-2	1-0	■	0-2	2-1	2-2	0-2	1-1	1-3	3-2	0-4
Gala Fairydean	1-0	2-3	0-2	■	2-0	3-1	5-0	1-0	2-0	2-2	4-2
Hawick Royal Alb.	1-0	1-7	4-1	2-3	■	5-1	1-1	0-1	1-1	3-3	1-3
Heriot-Watt Univ.	0-0	0-3	2-1	1-1	1-2	■	1-2	0-2	0-4	3-3	1-2
Kelso United	2-0	1-3	2-2	0-1	2-1	1-0	■	2-1	2-1	3-2	0-1
Pencait. & Ormis.	3-1	0-1	0-2	1-1	1-1	2-4	2-1	■	2-1	1-2	2-2
Preston Athletic	7-2	1-0	7-0	4-1	3-2	1-4	3-2	4-0	■	1-2	2-2
Selkirk	1-3	0-2	3-4	0-6	1-3	2-3	0-1	1-0	0-4	■	2-3
Threave Rovers	4-0	1-1	5-0	2-3	3-1	1-0	4-2	4-1	4-3	2-1	■

East of Scotland League

First Division Season 1999/200

Threave Rovers	20	15	3	2	55	26	48
Gala Fairydean	20	13	3	4	41	21	42
Kelso United	20	10	3	7	30	31	33
* Preston Athletic	20	12	2	6	58	29	32
† Edinburgh Univ.	20	11	2	7	39	22	32
Eyemouth United	20	8	3	9	27	44	27
Pencait. & Ormiston	20	7	4	9	24	29	25
Hawick Royal Albert	20	6	4	10	32	38	22
Heriot-Watt Univ.	20	4	4	12	26	42	16
Edinburgh Athletic	20	5	1	14	20	44	16
Selkirk	20	3	3	14	29	55	12

* Preston Athletic had 6 points deducted
† Edinburgh Athletic had 3 points deducted

Promoted: Threave Rovers and Gala Fairydean

92

31st March 1999
v CZECH REPUBLIC (ECQ)*Celtic Park*

Sullivan	Wimbledon
Weir	Heart of Midlothian
Boyd	Celtic
Lambert	Celtic
Elliott	Leicester City
Davidson	Blackburn Rovers (sub. Johnston)
Hopkin	Leeds United
Burley	Celtic
Jess	Aberdeen
McAllister	Coventry City (sub. Hutchison)
McCann	Rangers

Result 1-2 Jess

28th April 1999
v GERMANY *Bremen*

Sullivan	Wimbledon
Weir	Heart of Midlothian
Hendry	Rangers (sub. Ritchie)
Boyd	Celtic
Gemmill	Nottm. Forest (sub. Jess)
Durrant	Kilmarnock (sub. Winters)
Lambert	Celtic (sub. Cameron)
A. Johnston	Sunderland (sub. B. O'Neil)
Davidson	Blackburn Rovers (sub. Whyte)
Hutchison	Everton
Dodds	Dundee

Result 1-0 Hutchison

5th June 1999
v FAROE ISLANDS (ECQ) *Toftir*

Sullivan	Wimbledon
Weir	Heart of Midlothian
Boyd	Celtic
Calderwood	Aston Villa
Elliott	Leicester City
Davidson	Blackburn Rovers
Dodds	Dundee
Lambert	Celtic
Gallacher	Blackburn Rovers (sub. Jess)
Durrant	Kilmarnock (sub. Cameron)
Johnston	Sunderland (sub. Gemmill)

Result 1-1 Johnston

9th June 1999
v CZECH REPUBLIC (ECQ) *Prague*

Sullivan	Wimbledon
Weir	Heart of Midlothian
Boyd	Celtic
Calderwood	Middlesbrough
Ritchie	Heart of Midlothian
Davidson	Blackburn Rovers
Dodds	Dundee
Lambert	Celtic
Gallacher	Blackburn Rovers
Durrant	Kilmarnock (sub. Jess)
Johnston	Sunderland

Result 2-3 Ritchie, Johnston

4th September 1999
v BOSNIA (ECQ) *Sarajevo*

Sullivan	Wimbledon
Weir	Everton
Hopkin	Leeds United
Calderwood	Aston Villa (sub. Dailly)
Hendry	Rangers
Ferguson	Rangers (sub. Durrant)
Dodds	Rangers
Burley	Celtic
McCann	Rangers (sub. Gallacher)
Hutchison	Everton
Collins	Everton

Result 2-1 Dodds, Hutchison

8th September 1999
v ESTONIA (ECQ) *Tallinn*

Sullivan	Wimbledon
Weir	Everton
Davidson	Blackburn Rovers
Dailly	Blackburn Rovers
Hendry	Rangers
Durrant	Kilmarnock (sub. Ferguson)
Dodds	Dundee United
Burley	Celtic
Johnston	Sunderland (sub. McCann)
Hutchison	Everton
Collins	Everton

Result 0-0

5th October 1999
v BOSNIA (ECQ) *Ibrox*

Sullivan	Wimbledon
Weir	Everton
Davidson	Blackburn Rovers
Dailly	Blackburn Rovers
Hendry	Rangers (sub. Calderwood)
Lambert	Celtic
Dodds	Dundee United (sub. McSwegan)
Burley	Celtic
Gallacher	Newcastle United (sub. Burchill)
Hopkin	Leeds United
Collins	Everton

Result 1-0 Collins

9th October 1999
v LITHUANIA (ECQ) *Hampden Pk*

Gould	Celtic
Weir	Everton
Davidson	Blackburn Rovers
Lambert	Celtic
O'Neil	Wolfsburg
Ritchie	Heart of Midlothian
Dailly	Blackburn Rovers
Burley	Celtic (sub. Cameron)
Burchill	Celtic (sub. Dodds)
Hutchison	Everton
McSwegan	Heart of Midlothian (sub. Gallacher)

Result 3-0 Cameron, Hutchison, McSwegan

13th November 1999
v ENGLAND (EC Play-Off)
Hampden Park

Sullivan	Wimbledon
Weir	Everton
Dailly	Blackburn Rovers
Ritchie	Heart of Midlothian
Hendry	Rangers
Ferguson	Rangers
Dodds	Dundee United
Burley	Celtic
Gallacher	Newcastle United (sub. Burchill)
Hutchison	Everton
Collins	Everton

Result 0-2

17th November 1999
v ENGLAND (EC Play-Off)
Wembley

Sullivan	Wimbledon
Weir	Everton
Davidson	Blackburn Rovers
Dailly	Blackburn Rovers
Hendry	Rangers
Ferguson	Rangers
Dodds	Dundee United
Burley	Celtic
McCann	Rangers (sub. Burchill)
Hutchison	Everton
Collins	Everton

Result 1-0 Hutchison

29th March 2000
v FRANCE *Hampden Park*

Sullivan	Wimbledon
Telfer	Coventry City (sub. Johnston)
Davidson	Blackburn Rovers
Dailly	Blackburn Rovers
Hendry	Coventry City
Ritchie	Heart of Midlothia n(sub. Pressley)
Dodds	Rangers
Ferguson	Rangers
Gallacher	Newcastle United (sub. Burchill)
Hutchison	Everton
Cameron	Heart of Midlothia n(sub. McCann)

Result 0-2

SCOTTISH F.A. CUP 1999/2000

First Round

11th Dec 1999	Hamilton Academical	1	Clyde	2
11th Dec 1999	Huntly	0	East Stirlingshire	1
11th Dec 1999	Ross County	2	Forfar Athletic	2
27th Dec 1999	Threave Rovers	1	Stenhousemuir	7

Replay

3rd Jan 2000   Forfar Athletic 0   Ross County 0   (aet)
Forfar Athletic won on penalties

Second Round

8th Jan 2000	Albion Rovers	0	Dalbeattie Star	0
8th Jan 2000	Arbroath	0	Fraserburgh	0
8th Jan 2000	Brechin City	2	Annan Athletic	2
8th Jan 2000	Cowdenbeath	2	Clyde	3
8th Jan 2000	Dumbarton	0	Stenhousemuir	2
8th Jan 2000	Montrose	1	Queen of the South	3
8th Jan 2000	Partick Thistle	2	East Stirlingshire	1
8th Jan 2000	Peterhead	2	Forfar Athletic	1
8th Jan 2000	Queen's Park	1	Berwick Rangers	2
8th Jan 2000	Stirling Albion	2	East Fife	1
8th Jan 2000	Stranraer	1	Clachnacuddin	0
8th Jan 2000	Whitehill Welfare	2	Alloa Athletic	2

Replays

29th Jan 2000	Alloa Athletic	2	Whitehill Welfare	0
19th Jan 2000	Dalbeattie Star	1	Albion Rovers	5
15th Jan 2000	Fraserburgh	1	Arbroath	3
15th Jan 2000	Annan Athletic	2	Brechin City	3 (aet)

Third Round

29th Jan 2000	Albion Rovers	1	Partick Thistle	2
29th Jan 2000	Arbroath	A	Motherwell	A

Arbroath vs Motherwell was abandoned at half-time due to high winds

8th Feb 2000	Celtic	1	Inverness Caley Thistle	3
29th Jan 2000	Clyde	3	Raith Rovers	1
29th Jan 2000	Clydebank	1	Stirling Albion	0
29th Jan 2000	Dundee	0	Ayr United	0
29th Jan 2000	Falkirk	3	Peterhead	1
29th Jan 2000	Heart of Midlothian	3	Stenhousemuir	2
29th Jan 2000	Hibernian	4	Dunfermline	1
5th Feb 2000	Kilmarnock	0	Alloa Athletic	0
29th Jan 2000	Queen of the South	0	Livingston	7
29th Jan 2000	St. Mirren	1	Aberdeen	1
29th Jan 2000	Stranraer	1	Berwick Rangers	2
30th Jan 2000	Dundee United	4	Airdrieonians	1

Third Round (Continued)

| 30th Jan 2000 | Greenock Morton .... 1 | Brechin City .... 1 |
| 30th Jan 2000 | St. Johnstone .... 0 | Rangers .... 2 |

Replays

| 8th Feb 2000 | Aberdeen .... 2 | St. Mirren .... 0 | |
| 15th Feb 2000 | Ayr United .... 1 | Dundee .... 1 | (aet) |

Ayr United won on penalties

| 8th Feb 2000 | Brechin City .... 0 | Greenock Morton .... 0 | (aet) |

Greenock Morton won on penalties

| 19th Feb 2000 | Motherwell .... 2 | Arbroath .... 0 |
| 9th Feb 2000 | Alloa Athletic .... 1 | Kilmarnock .... 0 |

Fourth Round

20th Feb 2000	Inverness Caley Thistle 1	Aberdeen 1
19th Feb 2000	Greenock Morton 0	Rangers 1
19th Feb 2000	Alloa Athletic 2	Dundee United 2
19th Feb 2000	Berwick Rangers 0	Falkirk 0
19th Feb 2000	Clyde 2	Heart of Midlothian 2
19th Feb 2000	Hibernian 1	Clydebank 1
26th Feb 2000	Motherwell 3	Ayr United 4
19th Feb 2000	Partick Thistle 2	Livingston 1

Replay

29th Feb 2000	Aberdeen 1	Inverness Caley Thistle 0
22nd Feb 2000	Dundee United 4	Alloa Athletic 0
29th Feb 2000	Falkirk 3	Berwick Rangers 0
29th Feb 2000	Clydebank 0	Hibernian 3

Fifth Round

11th Mar 2000	Ayr United 2	Partick Thistle 0
11th Mar 2000	Hibernian 3	Falkirk 1
12th Mar 2000	Dundee United 0	Aberdeen 1
12th Mar 2000	Rangers 4	Heart of Midlothian 1

Semi-Finals

| 8th Apr 2000 | Rangers .... 7 | Ayr United .... 0 |
| 9th Apr 2000 | Aberdeen .... 2 | Hibernian .... 1 |

FINAL

| 27th May 2000 | Rangers .... 4 | Aberdeen .... 0 |

Van Bronckhorst, Vidmar, Dodds, Albertz

Attendance: 50,865

Statistics supplied by –

www.soccerdata.com